THE HORSE SENSE AND CENTS™ SERIES

TURNING CHALLENGING HORSES INTO WILLING PARTNERS

Nanette Levin

BookConductors, LLC
Rushville, NY

Published by:
Book Conductors, LLC®
www.BookConductors.com
(888) 875-3551

First Edition
Printed in the United States of America

Cover photographs © 2010 by David Crystal/Raspberry Hollow Photo

Publisher's Cataloging-in-Publication Data

Levin, Nanette.
  Turning challenging horses into willing partners / Nanette Levin.
  p. cm.
  ISBN: 978-1-61548-047-0

  1. Horses—Training. 2. Horses—Behavior. 3. Horsemanship. I. Title.

SF287 .L48 2009
636.1—dc22   2009907104

TABLE OF CONTENTS

FOREWORD

Nanette Levin is a *Through The Looking Glass* me; the anti-me, the me that I might be if it were as easy as going into a big walk-in closet full of "me's," skinning out of the one I'm in, selecting a different one hanging on the rack, and slipping into it as smooth as a favorite pair of jeans. Yep, I just might choose the Nanette Levin model if it were that easy.

Here's what I mean. If we were to lay our Equine Vitae side by side: Nanette's been riding horses for 40 years. Me too — the difference is, I rode about five times in the first 37 years, and now, I'm trying to make up for it.

Nanette breezes racehorses. I watch racehorses on TV. Nanette spends a lot of time at tracks, where her work with hot horses requires her to be a cool customer. I frequent tracks once every 3.62 years, place my two dollar bet, and get as excited over the outcome as if I'd mortgaged my house and put it all on a 50-to-1 longshot.

Last — perhaps most important — Nanette rehabilitates problem horses. No, make that "problemed" horses. The horses aren't the problem; what was done, or not done, with them before she gets them is the problem. And I? I am the happy-go-lucky owner and rider of a willing partner, started by people who did all the right things.

So why, you might ask, am I writing the foreword to *Turning Challenging Horses into Willing Partners*?

To let you know that anyone who spends time around horses can learn from this book. It's true, I've never personally ridden or handled the kinds of rogues, rascals and rapscallions that are Nanette Levin's bread and butter. Nevertheless, I devoured her stories, and you should too. If you're an amateur of any level working with horses, this book has immense practical value for you. If you're inexperienced with horses, as I was, you'll read Nanette's tales of Studley and Evil and big Bertha and realize where you should not be going, at least not without guidance and a darn good hospitalization policy.

There is no substitute for experience, and experience comes dear. There's no substitute, but Nanette's book is close. It distills her experience and that of ten other professional trainers into a readable and replicable method for dealing with problem horses. Even if you've always worked with horses in the "normal" range of crazy, you'll come away with ideas to fix those issues with your equine partner.

But, if you've come into possession of a true problem horse, or if you're considering working with more challenging mounts for some unfathomable reason, this book should be not in your library but in your barn. It should be required reading every day before you start your work, and every evening while you soak your sore muscles. If nothing else, it's likely to make some of your problems look tame by comparison. And because Nanette freely shares her mistakes as well as her successes, you won't feel intimidated by her level of expertise; you'll realize that even the pros don't do everything right the first time. Nanette teaches us that learning from our own (and others') mistakes can give us a second chance to get the job done.

There's a final group of readers who will benefit greatly from Nanette's horse sense. Nanette's *Turning Challenging Horses into Willing Partners* is to young-horse starters what Dr. Spock's *Baby and Childcare* is to new parents. None of us wants to be the person who turns out the kinds of problem horses Nanette works with at Halcyon Acres®, and if you read her book, you won't. You'll start to understand the things that can set a horse on the wrong path for life, and you'll avoid doing them. And if you don't, know that Nanette is there to fix them. But don't make her do that. Please.

ANGE DICKSON FINN
Columnist, "Last Laugh", Equine Journal
Author, *The In-Gate: A Parent's Guide to Horse Shows*

PREFACE

There's something to be said for learning from the wisdom — and mistakes — forged by others before you. The *Horse Sense and Cents*™ series is intended to help the novice identify problems and potential solutions, including solutions that may require professional assistance. The books are also designed to benefit the professional through lessons learned, case studies, and chapters that include insights of other equine authorities from around the world. The anecdotal approach of the series makes the reading fun and the material easy to implement.

While throwing money at a problem can be effective, it's more rewarding if you can understand what it takes to address or resolve an equine issue. Even if you choose to delegate training, raising, breeding, or any other activity that involves your horse (if you insist on spending the money, we at Halcyon Acres® welcome your business — visit us at http://www.HalcyonAcres.com), eventually you'll want to understand how your actions affect your horse's behavior.

For those who are living on a budget, but oh-so-determined to have a horse around the house or at a neighboring stable, we've been there and offer tips and tricks that can save you money and frustration as you dig your heels in to stay the course or gallop off into the sunset.

If you're looking for a down-to-earth, easy-to-follow, and imaginative guide to the equine challenges you face, this series provides an excellent tool for creative and effective solutions to what ails you or your steed.

We've chosen to feature our "turning" treatise as the first book because this is a concern almost every seasoned equestrian has faced, along with a good number of unfortunate novices to boot, yet it is a topic rarely covered in detail by the pros or the industry media. We use the term *turning* to explain the process of transforming a mount that has been taught to be uncooperative, scared, or mean into a willing companion. Usually, this is an equine that has been started badly and has major resulting issues that are the fodder for nightmares. Obviously, it's best to start right; but this doesn't always happen, and the ensuing quirks and behavioral challenges range from annoying to downright dangerous.

Our approach is different from the norm — we don't prescribe formula solutions but, instead, believe that each horse is distinctive in the way he or she responds and reacts to handler and rider cues. The signals and stories illustrated in this guide should help you identify problems that you may be facing with your steed while enabling you to type your horse a bit by recognizing tendencies. Identifying such behaviors may help you pinpoint how your horse may have been previously conditioned to distrust, disrespect, or hate his or her handlers and riders. The successful solutions can be guides as you strive to create an understanding between you and your particular problem child. Of course, we also offer mistakes as fodder for thought and cautionary notes on when it may be time to simply call it quits.

The time and effort necessary to turn a horse that's been conditioned to behave badly can be considerable, but the rewards associated with that moment of connection and rapport are immeasurable. Usually, the turn is sudden and dramatic. Additionally, if you are truly successful with your turning efforts, you will likely join with a mount that offers you a willingness to exceed your requests while sharing a bond that's more invigorating than any equestrian activity involving a made horse. I hope you are able to experience the joy of this amazing experience with your equine project.

NANETTE LEVIN

ACKNOWLEDGEMENTS

This book, and the others in the *Horse Sense and Cents*™ series, would not be possible without the collaborative effort of many who came forward to share their knowledge, networks, feedback, and stories.

Thanks to Heather Chaplin, Judie Framan, June Lattimore, Michele Metraux, and Gayle Sheehan for helping to identify some of the contributors in this book and making content suggestions.

Without the featured contributors in Section Three, this book would not be as rich an experience for the reader. A special thanks goes out to Dennis Auslam, Kels Bonham, Mike Bonham, Fleur Bryan, Denny Emerson, Robert Fera, Jutta Heinsohn, Claire Hunter, John Newborough, and Kathy O'Neal for their diverse knowledge, honest comments, and engaging stories of challenges and successes.

This book would not be as tight, clear, or pleasant on the eyes without the thoughtful feedback provided by Laurie Monroe to help fix some of the initial kinks in earlier stages of this manuscript as well as her creative skills and talent in designing the cover, the consulting and final proof support of Walt Shiel, the interior design expertise of Ariel Frailich, and the photo shoot by Dave Crystal that provided the cover images. It has been a wonderful team to work with, and I sincerely appreciate their considerable efforts to make this book a reality.

Finally, I would be remiss if I didn't give credit to the many horses that provided such a vast education and the ultimate inspiration for this book. The personalities, challenges, schoolings (often it was clear I was the one being trained), breakthroughs, quiet wisdom, reception, and willingness to consider new realities these horses offered will serve as memories to last a lifetime, and hopefully, great insight for the reader.

STARTING FROM A POSITION OF KNOWLEDGE

THIS BOOK IS DESIGNED TO address issues with horses that have already been started under saddle (albeit often to the detriment of any useful future training). Invariably, poor initial rider or handler training creates problem horses. Understanding why your mount is behaving badly is a smart start to fixing what ails him. Consequently, this section will help you understand what you're in for and offer some insights on how to identify the characteristics of typical problem horse types. If you're dealing with babies, or are starting a horse under saddle, look for our other books that deal specifically with these equine events.

Chapter One

THE CHALLENGE

PROBLEM HORSES TAUGHT TO MISBEHAVE — usually the case with bad actors — can try the patience of Job. Some are beyond help, but fortunately, many are reachable with some creative and persistent handling. The key is to be able to recognize the symptoms, craft a plan that addresses what ails them, and be inventive and flexible as you observe reactions. Often, you'll find it necessary to alter course to find an approach that works — today, but not necessarily tomorrow. The sad truth is, damage done can be minimized, but rarely completely reversed with horses that have been conditioned over time to view their human counterparts as adversaries. Sometimes, young horses caught early can be turned into clean and willing slates, albeit through a longer and tougher process than would be the case if they were started right in the first place. Still, we don't always have the choice to initiate our mounts properly, and it's not unusual to encounter a very talented or potentially kind steed that's worth the effort and risk to try to fix.

The word "turning" is a term we use at Halcyon Acres to describe a process whereby difficult and often dangerous mounts transform into willing, cooperative, and trustworthy steeds. There is often a sudden moment when the horse and human connect and the equine's attitude transforms from that moment forward. For equines that have been taught, whether intentionally or not, to fear, dismiss, or threaten their human counterparts, it is necessary to undo the damage. This can be achieved through a process of observation, consistent requests, and a patient and persistent approach. You want to encourage these animals to reject their former training and embrace a new cooperative demeanor that is more satisfying for all. If you respond to tantrums, evasions, and phobias in a manner the horse has grown to predict from prior poor handling, you encourage and ingrain these negative reactions. Instead, turning a horse requires an approach that fosters communication in both directions — and establishes you, the human counterpart, in a new realm as an understanding and responsive guide.

Rushed and overwhelmed steeds tend to fear new situations. Those who learn they can win through intimidation will seek to scare a rider or handler into compliance on their terms. Mounts conditioned to recognize that learning is painful often use violence in anticipation of a reaction in kind or flee when they do not understand. Learning to observe how your equine is reacting to situations and pinpointing a likely reason for the associated crazies is important as you begin to try to work through a strategy for success. Being able to adjust quickly as the horse responds to what you are asking (and realizing whether the approach is working or not) is critical in dealing with these critters. In most cases, determination will win out for either you or your project, but if you plan to be the victor, your strategy needs to be peppered with a savvy responsiveness that begins and pervades the entire turning process.

If you're game for a likely long process, but incredibly gratifying result, you may enjoy working with a challenging horse. Of course, having the skills and insight to work without a playbook helps. Even so, reaching a problem horse can be an unequaled experience — and if he does turn, he will do almost anything for you. So, results can be amazing, rewarding, and fun, but usually come only after you've invested a fair amount of sweat equity.

Chapter Two

IDENTIFYING THE ROOT
OF THE CHALLENGE

WHILE EACH CHALLENGING HORSE TENDS to react a little (or a lot) differently when offered the same guidance as another mount, much of his or her behavior can be traced to earlier handling. So, it's possible and practical to try to figure out a primary re-action mode and address it in your training regimen. Clearly, an adaptive and responsive approach to your equine's signals is the best method, but understanding his or her cues is critical in formulating an effective plan. Happily, there are some obvi-ous indicators that can clue you into what type of attitude you are dealing with.

Spend some time working on the ground initially with these horses — you can learn a lot from watching them, which is tougher to do when you are on their backs. Working in the stall on grooming and building rapport, then in the round pen or on long lines to begin establishing limits on what you will accept and demand, is a good way to start. This will give you some ob-vious and workable information to incorporate into your train-ing strategy.

Generally, you can reduce time involved in fixing problems with some effective groundwork that includes an observant eye and responsive hand and a system that lets you be the guide your horse is willing to accept. Of course, understanding why a horse is behaving badly is a critical step in this process.

SCARED STEEDS

Scared horses that have been conditioned to fear people are fairly easy to recognize. Their eyes bulge out of their heads with white often showing around the edges when they are alarmed. These steeds also tend to blow for no apparent reason. Addi-tionally, most have had their concerns reinforced with punishment, so their responses escalate after the initial misstep, getting even more dramatic as sheer terror occurs in anticipation of violent repercussions. Simply not reacting to the initial explosion and waiting out the subsequent drama with a steady and unflappable stance can do wonders in transforming these nervous creatures into reachable companions. Many label such horses as crazy, but the crazy behavior is often a product of fear that's been learned through former human contact. This type of fright is rarely an innate condition, so can usually be reduced or eliminated. Patience, understanding, and consistency are important with these equines.

MEAN MOUNTS

Mean equines are another story — but equally obvious, if not more so. Most have been taught to resent humans and conditioned to use violence to avoid pain. When they don't want to do something, it's usually communicated in very clear terms that involve pinned ears, active teeth, hoofs coming at you from many directions, rearing, and a variety of hostile acts designed to intimidate you at a minimum and, in harder cases, disable you.

If requests are frequently met with threats or actual violence from your project, you're probably dealing with a horse that has been turned mean. These horses need to be watched at all times, and caution must be a priority through each exercise. Don't lose sight of the fact that most mature horses probably have about a 1,000-pound advantage over you, and when they know it and are determined to use it to hurt the person they face, you'll never win by reacting in kind. Realize, too, that these animals are willing and capable of injuring you if you're not careful.

Fortunately, most mean horses can be turned with consistent and insistent training that puts you in control but not in peril. Regrettably, many of these mounts have also been soured in the process, and it is very difficult to fix a horse that has learned his only recourse to avoiding pain is to refuse. Of course, some mean horses you will never reach, without surgery anyway, including certain colts and mares that may have hormone issues (such as a cyst on an ovary with the latter), and products of bloodlines known for aggressive tendencies. A lot of times these types just aren't worth the hassle — or the risk.

AUTHORITATIVE ALPHAS

Alphas can be a riot, once you get into their heads and understand why they behave the way they do. They are also generally the hardest horses to turn after a bad start, but the most receptive if you do reach them. With Alphas, it's all about being in charge, and they don't take kindly to direction from someone they do not respect. Interestingly, discipline is rarely effective with these types. Staying power, instead, is the key. They will exhaust and exasperate you with their antics and determination to win. These horses also often try to bait you into losing your cool so that they have a reason to intensify the bad behavior and deem you an unworthy director. Yet, they can be the most satisfying projects to work with, if you are able to turn them. They melt when finally confronted with a leader they can comfortably follow.

Identifying an Alpha can sometimes be challenging as most are exceedingly smart and use ploys to convince you they are afraid, crazy, or confused so they can get their way. Still, most share some common traits that can be readily revealed if you know what to look for. Their true natures shine when they are pushed to complete a requested task. Whether it's leading on the end of a shank in a manner you deem appropriate, passing an obstacle, handling instruction when away from other horses, or tolerating a rider on their back (many learn early to dislodge riders and get very good at it), they get belligerent when pushed and may take hours of calm but steady insistence to complete a simple task willingly. They generally have a massive arsenal and will try another tactic when one stops working, with the same zeal for winning throughout the entire contest. The beauty of Alphas is, once you get through a particular issue, it's rare for this to ever be a problem again. The sudden and permanent transformation of the Alpha is an easy way to recognize them. If you've determined you are dealing with an Alpha, the communication process must start on the ground to be effective. You need to be able to watch and control these animals through a clear and calculated process that begins with body language not easily managed on their backs. They will tell you when it's time to proceed to under-saddle activities. Interestingly, most of the Alphas we've dealt with have been fillies.

TIMID TRIPS

Many blur the line between timid and scared horses, deeming them equals. They're not. Explosive, scared horses generally learn in early lessons that fear nets violent discipline from their handlers and are more concerned with what will happen after they spook or balk than they are of the initial cause for alarm. As noted earlier, the terror that ensues after the primary incident is a good clue in identifying a frightened horse. Timid horses, on the other hand, lack confidence but generally do not blow. They may spook or freeze in new situations, but they can be more easily coaxed to accept events with a confident and diligent hand. Usually, timid horses were rushed in early lessons and overfaced.

Many horses that refuse at fences or are unpredictable and wary on the trails are timid horses that have learned their riders or handlers can't be trusted to keep them out of harm's way. These equines also tend to tentatively approach new environments and can be unpredictable on the ground. While much of the work with these horses can be accomplished on their backs, no effort will be effective without an equestrian who can initially provide the confidence these horses lack through their demeanor and subsequently can ensure that the requests made of this mount are safe and reasonable for the horse's skill level.

SOUR SCOUNDRELS

Sour horses are pretty easy to identify — they refuse to do what you ask of them. This is usually accompanied by pinning their ears, planting themselves, whipping their tails or throwing hoofs in retaliation to requests, performing acrobatics designed to unload the rider, or exhibiting any other behavioral activity that communicates resistance. These are horses that have learned to hate training. Unfortunately, unless it's a mere matter of too much of the same routine or a soundness issue that has not been diagnosed and addressed, these characters are rarely good investments in time or money and often create headaches for their owners. Effective equine competitors enjoy the game, and forcing a horse that has come to view the challenge with disdain is rarely a good turning project. Still, if you are determined to try and reinvigorate a sour mount, we offer some stories and ideas in Chapter Seven.

DEVELOPING A WORK PLAN

Stories can help make learning easier. This is especially true when dealing with riding horses, a discipline that uses most of our senses, particularly when trying to turn a challenging mount. Therefore, the following chapters include instructional guidance with ample anecdotal information to illustrate some of the cases we've dealt with at Halcyon Acres. Working with equines that have learned to misbehave is always a trial-and-error process. We hope you'll discover a winning plan for your particular problem child with ideas from the many success stories, while also learning to exploit and avoid some of the mistakes we've learned from along the way.

Often, young horses are misunderstood during the "breaking" period and forced into situations that overwhelm, frighten, or annoy them due to the trainer's failure to communicate. This can last a lifetime, if these animals aren't reprogrammed — by restarting training from where things first went wrong. Caught early enough, these problems can be redirected for amazing performance results, but this process requires a lot of patience, staying power, and intuitive responses. There are few lost causes with horses, but a lot of lost opportunities due to misunderstandings. Problem mounts are more often the result of problem handlers and riders early in life, rather than inborn reactions. Get to know what your horse is trying to tell you, and you may be amazed at how much progress you can make with just a little bit of listening.

Chapter Three

WORKING WITH
SCARED HORSES

HORSES WHO HAVE LEARNED TO view human contact with terror are relatively easy to reach with a patient, consistent, and confident approach. It takes time, but teaching these over-reactive mounts to calm down and gain courage is certainly doable if the handler offers assurance through kind, safe, and steady guidance. The biggest issue with these horses is not the initial concern, but the escalated craziness that occurs as they anticipate the punishment for their fear. The best course of action when they blow, and then really blow, is to do nothing. Merely wait out the ordeal with a steady, patient, but insistent attitude that makes it clear you are not going to attack them for their fear but will not proceed until the tantrum ends. Generally, a willing attitude to proceed calmly and quietly ensues. Initial work off their backs is key for these characters, as you won't gain their trust while mounted until after you have been able to convince them that they need not explode when handled from the ground. Be careful and watchful, though, because you can easily be caught in a bad and dangerous position if you aren't ready for, and mindful of, their likely next move. Once you learn to read your horse, predicting his or her blow becomes relatively easy, albeit not foolproof.

INSTILLING SOUNDNESS OF MIND AND BODY

Nette needed some reprogramming. She had been broke, but arrived at the track as a nervous, erratic filly that had no self-confidence and little trust in riders or handlers. Her reactive behavior was likely a large contributor to some subsequent soundness issues that had her on respite by the summer of her two-year-old year. Bloodlines were considered a huge contributing factor, as the stud was known for producing crazies. She arrived at Halcyon Acres that winter.

Groundwork was critical in the beginning to reshape this filly's thinking and reaction to stressful situations. We spent a lot of time during her stay at the farm working on simple tasks in the stall with ample grooming and quiet contact that helped her learn to trust her human handlers. It was important to reassure this wary filly with calm and pleasant interactions with people. Making attention a welcomed treat versus a frightening experience was an easy initial and ongoing exercise for us and critical to Nette's continued progress. Each day, a good half hour of time was devoted to currying, brushing, combing her mane and tail, picking feet, and getting Nette used to being tied to the wall (a black rubber tie with double-ended snaps is generally best for this as it stretches quite a bit and will break when the situation gets dangerous) for happy handling in the stall. Seemingly simple tasks such as grooming, leading to and from the paddocks, and merely getting her into the routine of the facility were not so easy for Nette. She overreacted to everything and expected harm with each new experience. It was important to address Nette's anxiety with quiet and nonreactive time to prepare her for effective under-saddle work.

The second day Nette was at the farm, she spent a full twenty minutes rearing, nonstop, while being led home from the pasture. This was five feet from the barn entry door after calmly handling the trek from the paddock. We don't know what set her off, but it doesn't really matter. Ghosts, or imagined horrors only the horse can see from his mind's eye, are as prevalent in panic attacks as reasonable issues with these scared characters. Nette must have gotten perpendicular to the ground at least thirty times during this tantrum. Initially, she tried bolting toward the door each time her front feet touched the ground. She was eager to join the other horses, but quickly became consumed with terror over what would beset her after her instinctive move.

We stood our ground, but otherwise did nothing. Finally, she calmed down and willingly and quietly walked into the barn. That was the last time this leading issue surfaced. It was amazing to see this filly begin to transform after this single incident. Once Nette realized her reflexive, excited move wasn't going to prompt a beating, her fear subsided, she settled down, and she was willing to ponder a new paradigm.

Several factors were critical in making this incident so landmark for Nette. It was important that her fear was not reinforced with the aggressive reaction to rearing she was expecting. Doing so would have confirmed her expectations and reinforced the reactive, escalated behavior. Equally significant was the handler's ability to weather this tantrum with a quiet, fearless, patient, and steady response. Scared horses have a keen sense for when the people working with them are afraid and respond in kind with intensified reactions. In addition, it was critical to keep a hold of this filly without injury to either horse or handler. We always work with long lead ropes that are either leather or cotton to give ample room to deal with explosive situations and reduce the likelihood of a tendon injury or burn if the horse gets tangled in the line. When dealing with scared horses in particular, it is imperative to stay with them – whether on the ground or their backs. These equines rarely want to go it alone and tend to get more anxious when they're solo. They often run blind when released and can easily get hurt crashing through obstacles or running onto unsafe ground. Ensuring you maintain your contact with them (in a kind way) helps them calm down and gain confidence. With other types of horses, such as alphas or mean horses, a release would indicate a reward for their bad behavior. This is rarely the case, though, with scared horses, even though most have endured cruel or ignorant human handling.

Nette's behavior and demeanor as she walked off the trailer led us to suspect she was taught to be reactive, but this incident underscored the fact that her fear was, at least in part, learned, as she became more explosive after her initial outburst. This type of heightened response to a misstep is a key clue in determining when you are working with a scared horse.

We didn't even hop on Nette's back for two full weeks, instead opting for early handling and grooming lessons supplemented by training activities in the round pen. While we try to get out of the round pen as quickly as possible with a horse, we do find this space a great tool for horses that have had a communication breakdown with the people they've encountered. Nette was no exception. The circular nature of the space and required close proximity of the handler to the horse provides a useful environment to establish a connection. Body language is the first step to drive, encourage, or stop the horse. Putting yourself behind the horse's center drives them forward. Moving your body toward their shoulder or in front of their head (while in the center of the arena) should slow, stop, or turn them around. If you want them to accept your approach as non-threatening, turn your back to them (this helps with persuading them to stop, too).

Supplementing instructions that come from how you position yourself in this space with voice commands helps create a rapport with the horse to build on for later lessons. Be sure, when using voice commands, that the words you use and the tone of your voice for particular commands are consistent. In the round pen, it's relatively easy to keep the horse's attention on you. Of course, it's important to understand how your body position affects the horse's behavior and comprehension. Watch how your horse responds to where you are and what you do to get a sense for how much you may be unknowingly communicating. It's rare for a scared horse to intentionally misbehave, so don't be too quick to conclude a problem you are having is the horse's fault.

Our first week with Nette was spent merely trying to encourage her to walk quietly on the end of a longe line while being responsive to subsequent handler cues. Body language was particularly effective with this filly, and she understood and embraced movements that encouraged her to proceed, stop, stand, and maintain complete and confident focus on the handler by week two (see *Starting Young Horses* in our book series for a detailed discussion of body language in the round pen). This was no small task as this frightened filly's initial instinct was to accelerate to rapid speeds the moment she was given a little bit of line. Nette, however, was smart and eager to please.

Starting in very small circles is always best when trying to teach a horse to longe properly. This, coupled with the fact that the ground was a bit slippery at the time, helped discourage her from hitting her top speed. Each time we allowed her more line, she reacted with a quick retreat. Again, calm and patient encouragement to relax won out. By the end of the first week, she was ready, willing, and happy to quietly walk the perimeter of the round pen.

By this time, we had also established body language to enforce other aids (supplemented with the voice, which was a much tougher stimulus for her to process). This included stopping and standing until asked to proceed. To stop the horse, the handler moved slightly in front of her motion (while remaining in the center of the round pen) with her back toward the horse. To move the horse forward, the handler, facing Nette, positioned her body further and further behind the center of the horse to quicken her pace. Calm and quiet was far more important than speed, however, so the emphasis was always on slow and responsive behavior rather than faster gaits.

Once we hopped aboard, Nette trusted her human counterpart and was enthusiastic to learn and understand rider wishes. With two days under saddle in the round pen and then off to the trails, this filly, for the first time in her life, looked to her rider for reassurance and confidence. The two days riding her in the round pen were spent going from walk to halt and, at the end of the second session, a few strides at the trot. These under-saddle lessons lasted less than ten minutes, and were designed to give her confidence, reassurance, and quick praise for a job well done. All that was asked of her was to calmly move off the leg, turn, stop, and accept a rider as a nonthreatening presence. Lavish praise for simple tasks went a long way with this formerly overwhelmed filly.

For the first few days on the trails, we only traveled about 200 yards, turned around, and came home — all at the walk. By this time, she had come to accept and trust Gatsby, our 90-pound, white-and-black, canine assistant trainer. He had initially been banned from the round pen for training, but was brought in to track at her heels during later ground work exercises and early riding lessons. So, when anything new on the trail scared her, we brought him off her heels and sent him ahead. His safe passing, along with a rider who didn't react to her spooking, assured this tentative filly that she could proceed unscathed. In addition to calm, relaxed consistency when something strange-looking crossed her path, it was important to encourage this filly with a deep, quiet seat and a soft, encouraging hand and leg.

When dealing with a nervous or frightened horse, one of the most critical tasks for the rider is to relax. That includes loosening your knees and thighs and allowing your butt to sink deep into the saddle. Doing so can encourage the horse to move and (taking a deep breath usually helps here) assures the horse you are confident and able to lead him comfortably and safely over or around what concerns him. A deep seat allows you to feel and anticipate your horse's attitude. In addition, it provides a tremendous supplemental aid for everything from sending them forward (if done in a driving manner with seat bones deep in the saddle and your upper body slightly behind your hips) to stopping (with shoulders over hips over heels with a relaxed body and sinking seat) without the need for reins.

Using the seat to encourage a horse to be brave is underscored with a steady but gentle leg that releases the moment he proceeds, even a little bit.

The hands are there to guide and not to punish. As your horse encounters something that concerns him, make sure you are ready with the reins to keep him straight or guide him around obstacles. It's equally important to ensure you don't lose your balance and bang him in the mouth when he proceeds. When a horse is concerned, it's generally best to give him a longer rein to let him see and explore what frightens him. A tight rein also makes you tense and transfers that tension to the horse. It goes against instinct to loosen the hold when you are expecting a reaction, but tightening your grip will often cause the horse to be more worried and explosive.

Give your horse confidence with aids that tell him you are assertive, comfortable, and secure.

After of a few days of walk only on short trips up the trails, we introduced Nette to some jogging, or trotting, but only for a few strides to start. Nette was potentially explosive and extremely athletic, and our aim, early on, was to end every lesson on a win for both horse and rider. The quicker the better. There's nothing wrong with devoting five or ten minutes to a training session and quitting, if you can achieve a win and end on a good note. More time is not necessarily better, particularly with scared horses. If you push them too hard and they get frustrated or concerned, you'll lose a lot more ground and need to devote many more hours to regaining prior achievements than if you simply strive for short, simple, and successful lessons that let the horse excel in a single request.

Scared horses tend to learn best through praise. With early reprogramming, the reward includes an end to the session. However, that's not always possible. There were days we spent over an hour in the round pen with Nette, off her back, simply striving for a few walk strides with her eyes calm. On those days, the riding lesson was either skipped or abbreviated.

Sometimes, you need to compromise. If your equine is having a bad day and it becomes apparent you're not going to succeed in the lesson you planned, accept close enough and move on to an easier task. The key is to end with a response from your horse to your final requested task that's correct enough to justify praise. If that requires a change in the lesson plan, it's OK to shift the day's goal to something a scared horse can easily accomplish (but don't try this with an alpha and expect cooperation the next day).

We found with Nette that routine was important in her confidence building and comfort. So, for the first month on the trails, we started every day in the round pen. Here, she could respond to a familiar request with accuracy and ease, although sometimes the addition of tack and the anticipation of a rider made her nervous. Early on, this was on the longe line, striving for responsiveness and a quiet eye prior to proceeding, and could involve a considerable amount of time. Some days, we simply did a single turn, and she was ready. Regardless, we found even spending only a minute in the round pen at the start of the session saved possible hours of combating regression and associated difficulties. This was simply a filly that found comfort in a predictable pattern for training, and it was no big deal to accommodate this preference.

Over time, we extended the miles and added longer jogs and short gallops. Mostly, though, our pace was at the walk as this was the toughest gait for this filly to handle, and calming her down was an important goal. We did experience some tantrums coming home when a walk was demanded, but she ultimately understood this was nonnegotiable and complied. Of course, by this time, we had pretty much eradicated the crazies, and her behavior on this one was all about impatience and had little to do with concern. It was important to set this limit given what would be required when she went back to the track.

At first, fear netted some pretty dramatic reactions with Nette — and her leaps and spins did make it challenging for the rider to maintain a normal heart rate at all times — but once she realized the rider would not put her in harm's way, she gained confidence in herself and was eager to tackle new challenges.

Any form of punishment with this rattled filly was necessarily avoided as she blossomed into a kind, relaxed, eager pleaser.

Dealing with Nette taught us a lot, particularly relating to foals sired by her stud. We had occasion to work with a number of older offspring (most already running and too far-gone to reach in the confines of the track environment) prior to dealing with this filly, but she provided the key to their crazies. What we discovered — and this has consistently been a factor in subsequent horses from this bloodline — is that these youngsters are slow learners that can't deal with new lessons until a prior one is understood and mastered. If they're rushed through early handling or under-saddle activities, it blows their minds and, if not corrected, they act crazy for the rest of their careers.

Interestingly, a little bit of patience and a whole lot of customized attention to their training needs can transform these potentially explosive, unpredictable, and dangerous steeds into willing, cooperative, and keen performers. We determined that insistence or correction didn't work well with these horses, and the only way to reach them was by focusing on and rewarding accomplishments. We also came to recognize that these youngsters are best handled by a single person that they can come to trust. Consequently, we decided almost immediately to forego any ground assistance with Nette, instead opting to have only one person responsible for all initial handling and riding work. This proved to be a very successful approach for her. We will continue to do so with future starts or turning projects from this stud. There are certainly sires out there with a justified reputation of producing crazies. In this stud's case, though, it seems the handlers are more to blame for the outcome than the horse. Regrettably, earlier different handling of this filly would have probably completely altered her fate.

Those who had handled and ridden Nette the prior year were amazed at her transformation after we brought her from the farm to begin training again at the track. Once the bad memories were confronted and addressed over the first week or two, this eager filly morphed into a kind, quiet, and gracious pleaser who not only became a preferred morning mount for exercise riders and jockeys alike, but also a favorite of the grooms. She proceeded to race day with a previously illusive soundness throughout the rigors of her training regimen designed to prepare her for the event.

This volatile-turned-amicable filly showed talent that became increasingly apparent through her renewed, enchanting personality. She was one of the special ones who will be sorely missed.

HORSE SENSE WITH SCARED EQUINES

• Be calm, patient and nonreactive.

• Recognize their fear is more about anticipated human conduct than environmental issues that prompt the initial response.

• Slow down the lesson demands and ensure they are comfortable and confident with a single request prior to proceeding to the next.

• Never punish them for being afraid – instead, stand your ground and reassure them you are a competent and trustworthy leader by being steady through their tantrums.

• Lavish them with praise for tackling a challenge.

• Be unflappable. If you are afraid of your horse or concerned about introducing them to new tasks, get someone else to help you through the initial process. Scared horses can become dangerous to their handler and themselves if they sense a nervous human.

• Make groundwork the training stage to set the foundation for any riding accomplishments. These critters need to trust you first, and this is best done with body language and quiet and confident handling.

• Try to ensure early turning exercises involve only a single handler/rider. Scared horses have lost trust in humans and adding other people to the mix increases their anxiety. It's best to build their confidence with a single person they can learn to depend on, appreciate, and please.

• Always try to find ways to address learning exercises with reward vs. discipline.

• Keep lessons as short as possible and focus on a single issue and an easy win.

• Adapt your approach to the horse's needs by listening to find comfortable activities for communication and rapport.

• Enjoy even the smallest achievement and know that appreciating and rewarding this will provide huge dividends in the future.

Chapter Four

TURNING MEAN TO GREEN

MOST MEAN HORSES ARE SMART. They've learned, through on-going provocation, to terrorize human counterparts who have taught them to resent training. Granted, some are born mean with bloodlines being the cause, but most are conditioned to behave badly through a trial–and–error process where they find viciousness their sole recourse to alleviate agony.

BERTHA

Bertha came to us as a transition project, having served as a former hard-knocking racehorse, and more recently, an intended broodmare. After a two-year period of nothing but pasture time, we got the call for the career change. A cyst was discovered on her ovary that would require an operation for any possible success in breeding attempts. The owner had recently died, and the widow decided not to invest in the operation. She shipped Bertha to Halcyon Acres to be retooled as a riding horse. The cyst also affected her behavior — in bigger ways than we had initially imagined. This growth ultimately presented considerable issues on the ground, although we were able to correct problems under saddle.

The agent handling the mare warned us she was nasty, aggressive, and destructive, but her lovely gaits, large-boned frame, and size made her a good prospect for competitive arenas, particularly as a dressage performer. We also wanted to start her over fences to determine her proclivity for jumping and to explore other possibilities for this mare.

The first month was a nightmare. While we were able to deal with some of the socialization issues by pasturing her with our clever lead pony Porky, handling and under-saddle challenges were immense. She was vicious in the stall, leaving a bruise on a handler's arm the size of a grapefruit, after a bite with no cause. She shattered boards in the stall as she lambasted the walls because feeding wasn't quick enough, or the turnout routine didn't suit her, or simply because she felt a need to intimidate the horse next to her. She charged a naive photographer, teeth bared, as he entered the pasture, uninvited and unaccompanied, thinking he could slip in to capture images of this mare. She couldn't even walk a twenty-meter circle sans rider, without falling toward center, because she was so unbalanced.

Bertha's meanness was evident on the ground, but we were curious to see if this would also be an issue with under-saddle training. This wasn't a mare that would be fixed by groundwork as her behavior was induced by the cyst, and the owner and agent were in a hurry to find her a new home.

We jumped on her back the day after she arrived and realized there were more problems than we had anticipated. We discovered she was so herd-bound that you couldn't even get her attention for a moment, let alone a response to the leg to move forward, nor the hands to steer, as she screamed and ignored any rider aids in her singular focus on seeing and talking to other horses. This was peculiar because we discovered during her stay that this mare had no interest in other horses, except to beat them up, when loose in the paddock. We spent the next hour and a half merely working to gain control as we tried to walk from the round pen to a larger riding arena. This was all done on her back and through unwavering insistence that she proceed politely in the direction requested.

Part of this mare's intent was to intimidate the rider into giving up and getting off. Attitude can be a huge factor in turning these types, and being able to respond with fearless yet calm insistence helps a lot. We were able to end this lesson on a positive note by incorporating a deep seat, a leg that released as she proceeded and pressed when she froze, spun or resisted, and a hand on the ready to keep her moving in the right direction, but soft and quiet between tantrums.

Fortunately, Bertha was pretty good at retaining lessons, and we found once a battle was won under saddle (and in her case, responding quickly and clearly to her nastiness in kind was effective, the converse of Studley, featured below), it was rarely revisited. Bertha probably had quite a bit of Alpha in her, but it was initially so overshadowed by the meanness, it was tough to tell. The agent freely admitted she hated this mare, and it's possible some of her behavior was the result of hostile handling and/or limited correctional contact.

By day three, we had her paying attention to the rider instead of the other horses on the property. This process took a lot of time, but involved some pretty simple, commonsense tactics and perseverance. Once the tack went on, Bertha decided she wanted to be with, or at least see and talk to, company. The only way that was going to happen for her was if she complied with our requests. So, we initially isolated her from all horses on the property during training sessions by putting the rest of the herd in the barn. We worked at each basic task until she stopped screaming and spinning before proceeding to the next. Once she became willing to advance to the arena properly, we asked for brief attention and a positive response to a particular lesson. Then, it was quitting time and she was turned out as a reward for her compliance. The next step (with equal challenges) was to have her focus on rider cues while other horses were in the paddocks. She had the same initial hysterical tantrums, but learned quickly these would not be rewarded. Over time, she realized that any behavior that focused on other horses instead of the rider netted longer lessons. Rider attention met with a quick end to the workout. She was smart enough to understand what she needed to do for the reward system to kick in.

Bertha was basically lazy, certainly unfit, and unaccustomed to using her muscles properly. We later learned she had been turned out in a paddock on a very steep hill with little room to run, so this was probably a contributing factor to her physical challenges. When we used our leg or seat to try to correct her carriage, she reacted by aiming her hind hoofs at the rider aboard. She pinned her ears, tried planting herself, turned to bite the rider's leg, and exhausted an arsenal of evasion tactics prior to acquiescing. This was merely in response to a request to proceed properly at the walk. Our goal was to spend about ten minutes per session for a responsive demeanor. That rarely occurred, and the early lessons lasted a lot longer than we would have liked. As soon as she proceeded willingly and somewhat balanced, we quit.

This mare was talented and worth the effort to try to convert to a new career. We spent more than four months with simple balance, rhythm, transition, and attitude challenges focused on dressage basics and, ultimately, some schooling over fences.

Bertha was originally too big, too unbalanced, and too belligerent to make work in tight spaces productive. She wasn't very happy on the trails either and time spent here was not fun for the horse or rider. Safety was also a concern because when she decided to blow, it didn't seem to matter to her if the footing was bad or the incline steep or whether her thrashing, flinging, or rearing could send her tumbling into dangerous territory.

We decided to work with her in a one-acre rectangular wood board paddock that was on a slight incline. The terrain actually helped in that she had no sense of rhythm and merely climbing and ascending the very slight hill representing the short length of the paddock forced her to seek help from the rider. Most of our under-saddle time was spent in circles, serpentines, and figure eights, first at the walk and—once bending, balance, and responsiveness became easier for this mare—at the trot. Canter came into the mix after a month or two, but was only worked on a few days a week. As soon as she picked up a correct lead with a proper transition in each direction (some days we only worked on her better lead, particularly if her mood was a bit sour), we stopped that day's request for this gait.

During our lessons, each time she responded correctly for a few strides to a bend request, she was rewarded with a longer rein and a straight line.

While Bertha ignored the leg and the hand at first, she was responsive to the seat and learned to appreciate the help this provided in getting her better balanced and assisting her in establishing a consistent cadence. In a short period of time, once she got her mind on business, Bertha became very soft in the mouth and responsive to light leg cues. It seems her no-reply approach to the rider during the first week or so had nothing to do with deadened sides or a hard mouth, but was merely Bertha choosing to ignore the aids. Once we got past this stage, she was actually incredibly agile on cue, particularly for such a big horse.

The biggest issue with this mare was balance and the associated proper carriage to achieve it. Consequently, the bending work was critical in teaching her to engage her hind end, lighten in front, and develop a cadence. Bending her around the inside leg on the turns and supporting her with an outside leg slightly further back, to keep her right and help with steering, was very effective in improving all of her responses. As her muscling and balance improved, her attentiveness increased and transitions became seamless.

The initial concern, namely eliminating the meanness, was a relatively easy task under saddle, once she understood that rewards came when requests were met. Bertha wasn't a typical mean horse, in that her attitude stemmed from a physical issue (the cyst) that made her hormones go haywire. Over time, we found there was little we could do about her destructive behavior during nonriding hours. Fortunately, she learned to enjoy training and the activity gave her (and us) a respite from the chemical issues that made her difficult during the rest of the day.

Interestingly, Bertha was willing and kind jumping over fences — too much so, as her easy and enthusiastic approach to jumps had her tackling obstacles with no concern for injury as she crashed through poles at the trot. As we progressed with under-saddle training, we came to realize the extent of this mare's talent. Once she understood aids and desired responses, this huge mare could modify the length and/or cadence of her stride dramatically and in an instant. Sometimes, you need to look past the annoying issues to see the potential.

We never were able to resolve some of Bertha's pasture issues. Porky's getting older, and we tired of Bertha's continued aggressiveness toward this amiable alpha mare; so we decided to give Bertha a schooling by turning her out with our 14.3-hand broodmare Midge, whom we knew would be gentle unless provoked. Unfortunately, even after this mare attacked Midge and paid for it with injuries that required a month-long layup to heal, she failed to learn from the schooling. She continued to try to engage Midge in battle, but never got smart enough to realize she was always the loser. We decided it wasn't worth the trouble or cost of giving her company, so she now gets turned out alone.

Bertha can still be aggravating on the ground and does require occasional correction for unacceptable behavior, but responds better than she used to and has come a long way from her overtly dangerous days. She now shines under saddle and this makes some of her quirks in the stall and pasture more palatable. She continues to lambaste stall walls on the occasions when she can't get with the program. This apparent penchant causes periodic, senseless injuries. Bertha will likely never be a horse you would cozy up to as a gentle, intuitive, and cuddly friend, but she could be an outstanding performer in the right hands.

Sometimes, simply being able to recognize what allows a horse to shine and accepting the things you'll never be able to change is enough to enjoy what a horse can offer. In Bertha's case, we'll be glad to see her leave our farm, where fitting in with the crowd and embracing the routine is a requisite for long-term tenants. Still, we imagine her new owner will find her a delightful performer and a welcome companion — particularly if she's stabled at someone else's facility. It is amazing with this mare how easily and adeptly she embraced under-saddle work and came to eagerly enjoy the lessons. Daily riding definitely improved her demeanor in the stable, so it's likely an owner focused exclusively on this mare will be able to reach her in ways not possible at this farm.

STUDLEY

Studley seemed like a lost cause the moment he walked off the trailer. The owner was adamant about keeping him a stallion, even though he was vicious, horny, and unruly. He had put a groom in the hospital three days prior to arriving at Halcyon Acres by breaking his face with no cause. He refused to train during the three attempts with two different riders and a lead pony at the racetrack. Even the trucker, who was tough as nails, delivered the horse with considerable warnings and a conviction that this horse was unreachable. Studley had already raced, but had turned sour, mean, and out of control. This wasn't his fault — he was sore and likely forced to train over his objections before he retaliated. That didn't make him any less dangerous.

On the first day, merely leading him to the pasture was a perilous activity. The first five days of handling this horse were done only after a lip chain was secured prior to even entering a stall or pasture. He was a terrible striker, biter, and rearer, and was dead set on drawing blood from any human he encountered. An iron halter netted some control for two days, until he learned to ignore it like every other device designed to get his attention. We spent a week handling him with these tools combined, plus a longe whip, merely to avoid an ambulance call during leading and basic handling requisites in early turning sessions. Success was questionable.

We began working with him in the round pen with a lip chain attached to the longe line and a twenty-foot whip. He came at us with teeth, front feet, back hooves, and a vengeance. The key to this horse was controlling his behavior without getting into a battle of strength or nastiness — he clearly had us beat on both fronts. The round pen was an ideal environment to start a positive communications process. We also worked on identifying, treating, and addressing his soundness issues with an exercise plan to help strengthen areas that were weak and provide low-impact workouts to create a solid and sound foundation for future demands.

After a few days on the line working on voice commands and restraint, we turned him loose with merely a 20-foot longe whip for protection. Interestingly, the only thing he seemed to initially respect and respond to was the motion and noise of the whip. When using a longe whip with any horse, the objective is not contact, but behavioral control. He tried attacking the handler repeatedly, but the contained round pen space and ability to "drive" him with body language and the aid of the whip behind his forward motion worked well to establish safety and foster communication. It's likely that actual contact with the whip on this beast would have provoked a vicious attack, although the idea of using it as a weapon if necessary was certainly a consideration. Fortunately, it didn't come to this as he respected the sight and sound of the device enough to retreat when matters were verging on perilous. Merely controlling the direction he traveled, demonstrating a lack of fear (sort of — this horse was honestly terrifying for the first week or so), and maintaining a determination and structure to guide the horse until he acquiesced, transformed his temperament.

Surprisingly, the meanness toward his handler dissipated completely by day ten, and he willingly tolerated a rider mounting with a stirrup, standing patiently until instructed otherwise. (This was another one we decided to handle without any ground help — for very different reasons than Nette, including likely hospitalization of the help, potential related cancelled insurance coverage, and, more importantly, the safety of the rider. This was a horse looking for a fight and two people at once would have signaled a challenge for him to meet with violent glee.) Interestingly, Studley came to welcome his human handler — nickering hello and lowering his head at chest level hoping for a vigorous pet. He became a quiet and kind equine in the stall and round pen, although he continued to be dangerous in hand as hormones ruled when other horses came into the mix. Still, routine became something he embraced. While explosions, leaps, and striking while on the lead became a predictable daily event, once he transitioned from a necessarily isolated treatment to a part of the regular schedule at the farm, we learned to tolerate some of this excitement in deference to his newfound kindness on other fronts — and with the knowledge that if we pushed too hard to cure his outbursts, we'd lose considerable progress elsewhere.

Of course, the initial cited offense with this horse was his refusal to train — an attitude probably developed with good cause. Once the vicious behavior was redirected, we started tackling the next problem, his conditioned dislike for training. This horse was ready and willing to engage in battle. In fact, he was artful at baiting the rider to be forceful so that he could retaliate. It was important with Studley to ask without relenting or showing any fear, but to refrain from physical discipline. The meanness was now latent, but at the ready if a rider reacted in any way to justify its resurrection.

Within two weeks, we were tackling the trails, slowly at first, and increasing the pace as he consented. Interestingly, we found this horse to be most comfortable with a pattern, in paths and requests that were constant. So, instead of the typical sour-horse approach of mixing it up to stave off boredom, we tried to stick with a regimen to keep him happier. Any deviation from predictable repetition brought his acerbic proclivities to the fore, with a dangerous, lengthy, and frustrating standoff where progress was unattainable, but compliance was necessary, so that we didn't lose ground.

One of the most telling, scary, yet intriguing sessions with this colt was when we got the stupid idea of moving his training to our two-mile loop, which required crossing a running stream toward the back of the property.

Studley doesn't like water. Now we know.

Unfortunately, once he was introduced to the request, it was critical that we won this one, or the progress that we had made in gaining a respectful and sometimes-compliant attitude from this horse would be lost. We spent more than two hours trying to coax and, later, threaten him to cross the stream. At first, we did the standard patient wait until he was ready to proceed, but that merely made him more willful and convinced of his power.

We tried encouraging him by sending Gatsby (our canine assistant trainer) ahead to show him how easy and painless it was to cross. We hopped off his back and tried leading him over the stream. Leading didn't work — how about backing? Forget about it — that was more dangerous and violent than being on his back. Studley was too smart and too determined to be fooled into this trick and his reaction was scary as he started rearing and striking at the handler and then charging at her. Studley's downhill position was the only reason he wasn't able to strike a debilitating blow and gain freedom to travel to another county. Frustration won out and stupidity started to rule as we tried disciplining him into compliance. Bad move. Everything else we could think of was thrown into the mix, but ultimately, he got himself so caught up in the trees and brush surrounding the water after we remounted that the only way he could extricate himself was to get to the other side. A bit of dumb luck won out in this case.

Now what? Obviously, crossing back was not something he would do agreeably, and the prospect of another two-hour session wasn't particularly enticing. Exhaustion was a big factor, as was waning patience. Perceived brilliance quickly turned to regret as we left the 120 acres of property we knew to avoid another battle and became hopelessly lost. Since this whole debate started around noon, we didn't even have the sun as a guide because there was no telling the direction we had wandered away from home. Gatsby ditched us before we realized how lost we really were, opting for a stream crossing toward home. While this stud willingly followed the path he was led toward — sometimes under saddle and other times in hand over obstacles including logs, thick brush, tight trees, and belly-deep swamps, he continued to balk at any crossing that involved running water, sending us further away from any possible right heading. We were trapped in dense woods and the sun was setting fast. Studley knew we were in trouble and passively handled barriers that he ordinarily would have considered impassable. Somehow, we found some familiar turf and made it home, but not without a lot of anxiety.

This incident demonstrated Studley's willingness to forgo his mean streak. This horse had ample opportunity to disable and ditch his rider, but chose not to. That was reassuring and, frankly, a source of pride relative to the accomplishment and the horse. What was amazing was how this belligerent foe turned into a team player during this crisis. The horse could definitely be reached in dire circumstances, which provided some wonderful insight and an optimistic view toward future training.

It didn't last.

Studley continued to be a sour and stubborn mount and delighted in taunting and goading his rider to elicit cause to release the devil inside him. While he'd gallop on the farm and we could traverse the necessary miles to get him fit, it had to be on his terms, and the routine was critical in gaining his cooperation. Instead of trucking him to the track for preliminary training, we kept him at the farm to put miles and some limited speed work into him until he was ready for a recorded morning workout (or breeze) at the racetrack. This proved an important strategy as Studley arrived at the track with his meanness under control, but belligerence still intact.

It is common to start a breeze from one of the poles situated inside the rail along the interior perimeter of the racetrack. These are timed and documented sprints that serve to help get a horse fit for race day and offer handicappers a morning performance record that may help them (or not) determine which horses are likely to be top finishers in afternoon races. These color-coded poles designate the distance to be traveled to the wire, or what would be the finish line in a race. Working from the pole wasn't very effective on Studley's first intended breeze — he bolted and slammed on the brakes. The trainer suggested breaking from the gate with company as an alternative. This proved to be a great approach and served him well as a regimen up to race day. (Studley had certainly demonstrated that routine was his preferred MO.) Morning galloping was often a forty-five-minute ordeal as he refused to go on the track, planted himself, resorted to backing up at a dizzying pace, and made the three-eighths gap once we turned him around. After his rebuttal routine, however, he proceeded willingly and eagerly, managing to complete necessary training between trips to the starting gate.

Studley will always have control issues. However, a creative, unrelenting, yet soft approach to gaining little wins in short time periods, teaching him that a handler need not be the enemy, and sometimes compromising with him to avoid a battle has transformed him into a useful and less homicidal mount. Enforcing his conviction that people were to be hated with harsh demands would have been fruitless. Of course, he'll try the patience of the biggest pacifist, but a handler's succumbing to frustration always turns to regret with this colt, given the ensuing extra time required to reschool Studley and regain lost ground.

On the win side, Studley ran second in each of his five subsequent starts at the track against allowance company, racking up a pretty good sum in purse money. His meanness was not at the fore during the racing season in New York, but we knew it could be quickly resurrected with impatient handling. His sour approach to training will likely never be resolved, but we hoped he'd prove a winner regardless.

HORSE SENSE WHEN DEALING WITH MEAN EQUINES

• Mean horses are extremely dangerous and require careful, observant, and skilled handling. Most are pleased to hurt you and have been taught to loathe human interaction. Do not expect kindness alone to turn them into affectionate and willing partners. The first step for your welfare (and theirs) must be to establish an unwavering and fearless leadership position.

• Violent horses do not generally respond well to discipline. In fact, physical contact that is combative will often encourage them to show you just how mean they can be – and how much bigger and stronger they are than you. Assertiveness is important, as is control, but make sure this is done with body language and attitude, and not abuse.

• Beginners and novice riders should never attempt to handle mean horses without a more experienced hand at the ready. These horses want to hurt you (and have usually been given just cause for such an attitude) and require seasoned guidance.

• When a mean horse responds, even a little bit, to a request that has been a challenge in the past, ensure you release the pressure immediately to provide a reward. The only way you will turn these horses is to teach them how to have a happier life with humans. If you don't immediately acknowledge even the smallest effort to respond in a kinder fashion, they will lash out, as you will underscore their conviction that humans are the enemy.

• Mean horses tend to turn quickly. Isolating them and making you their only available friend helps. Ensuring your contact with them is nonthreatening, rewarding, and controlling is critical. If you are getting nowhere and/or going backward after a few weeks, change your approach, get some help, or give up.

• It is common for mean horses to revert to old habits the moment you threaten them. Try to avoid losing your temper with these critters.

• Lessons need to start on the ground with mean horses. It is extremely difficult to establish a communications foundation on their backs. Make sure you have created a connection and respect prior to trying to tackle riding challenges.

• Rule out physical issues prior to beginning work. Horses often turn mean due to pain. It is unlikely you will be successful turning a mean horse until you eliminate the source of this suffering.

• Praise can go a long way with mean horses, once they become receptive to change. Determine what your project finds pleasing (a pat, a treat, turnout, the trails, a toy – it can be anything) and use the tool lavishly to reinforce good behavior.

• Use your voice to reinforce cues, but be consistent. Your words and your tone can go a long way toward beginning a clear communications process with a mean horse.

Chapter Five

AN A FOR EFFORT COMES WITH ALPHAS

SOME OF THE TOUGHEST FOUGHT battles are the most rewarding. Interestingly, it seems the most determined cases, able and willing to wear you out to the point of giving up, acquiesce right about the time you're ready to walk away. These are almost always Alphas and will make you earn their respect — with the bruises to prove it.

Alphas are idiosyncratic horses to deal with and are fairly easy to recognize. They are also your most likely — albeit toughest — cases to turn. Most rule the pasture, and the strong ones have yet to encounter a horse or person who has stood their ground with them long enough to persuade them to "listen." Once they find an animal or a person that has the staying power to earn their respect, they often soften and relish the opportunity to have a leader. These horses usually turn instantly and dramatically when they acknowledge you are a worthy guide. They also tend to be extremely willing, predictable, dependable, and outstanding performers who aim to please those they esteem — to extremes. Of course, getting there is no easy task.

Usually, discipline and hostility toward an Alpha is a mistake. Never back down; instead, demonstrate your power by holding your ground and remaining calm, fearless, and insistent as they launch a bevy of scare or avoidance tactics at you. Typical young Alphas will throw tantrums anytime they are asked to comply with a request that doesn't suit them. They can be kind, smart, and compliant foals for early handling and lessons they find interesting, engaging, or fun. Once they are asked to respond to a request that isn't on their agenda, however, they can turn into monsters. Those that are effective at intimidating a novice or tentative early handler into compliance tend to be difficult horses to start under saddle. If the attitude isn't rectified in early under-saddle activities, it escalates, and these animals become problem children who need reprogramming if they are to be safe and honest mounts.

ATHLETE BABY OF THE DECADE RETURNS
AS BRONC CHAMP RE-BREAK

Jay merits mention in both our *Turning Challenging Horses* and *Don't Get Thrown Starting Horses Under Saddle* books because she was a dual challenge that came to Halcyon Acres for initial starting (which wasn't completed) and then back to fix her subsequent, learned talent for unloading riders at another farm that tried, albeit unsuccessfully, to take her on.

We were making good headway with this difficult Thoroughbred filly during her first stay at the farm, having gotten to the point where she was accepting a rider on her back and handling some basic leg, seat, and hand commands at the walk indoors, but were far from finished when the owner made a decision to stop for reasons that were not related to training efforts. Jay left, but the owners were given a dire warning concerning future handling and an advisory to keep others off her back until she returned for finishing.

She came back all right, but it wasn't until after another tried to "start" where we left off and managed, in the process, to reinforce her penchant for winning — effectively launching and terrorizing anyone who dared hop on her back. Taking her back was a tough call. One of the things we had avoided in early training was giving this filly any reason or opportunity to use her athleticism to unload a rider. She didn't during the time she spent at the farm, but it required very careful and observant handling. We knew, if she learned how to use her extraordinary ability and determination to unseat her mount, that even an extremely able rider would have a tough time sticking with her. Yet, we also saw the tremendous, albeit latent, talent she possessed and were convinced if it could be channeled, she would become an impressive performer. The owner contacted us with a query on what to do — just about convinced she wasn't worth the trouble and ready to log her as a lost cause. With no guarantees, we persuaded him to try one more time to see if the filly could be reprogrammed and properly prepared for a racing career.

When she arrived, we spent some time working with her off her back in the stall and round pen to try to reestablish some ground rules. These she accepted pretty readily and easily, having recalled earlier lessons (a typical trait of Alphas is that they retain information seemingly forever — good or bad — and it's rarely necessary to revisit a successful session).

Once we introduced a rider into the mix, the big problems began. Reprogramming can go both ways — and in her case, what she had learned during her absence was extremely detrimental to the forward progress initially established under saddle. We decided to start in the stall to limit her movement and reduce the likelihood of her getting up enough room or speed to launch her passenger. Yet, she was now accustomed to a routine that included a triumphant lesson with a swift dump in the dirt for anyone who straddled her back. She was quickly aggravated with the new approach that made it tougher to unseat the rider and immediately began to integrate new tricks. It took her less than two days, after exhausting her developed arsenal unsuccessfully and throwing a whole lot of new ideas at the problem, to learn to rear and flip over backwards. With this development, it was too dangerous to continue in the stall, and we moved to the round pen.

Often, with Alphas, it's best to work with them one-on-one. We found this an effective early strategy with this filly, so decided to forgo a handler at her head for the move to outdoor riding. For about a week, we bellied over her first, watching her eye closely and dismounting prior to the blow, and then, as she accepted a rider across her back quietly and willingly, put a leg over her other side and sat up. During the first few days (these lessons were anywhere from one to two hours in length), simply standing and accepting a rider was a sufficient note to end on. As the week progressed (although the time involved for the lessons remained lengthy), we added walking and stopping on cue to the mix. The mere addition of movement added some athletic explosions to the sessions and, ultimately, we decided it would be best to try to proceed with a lead pony as a companion before she learned again that her gyrations and gymnastics could dislodge her passenger. She had been exposed to our lead pony, Porky, during her prior stay (albeit without a rider) and appeared to enjoy the activity, and so it seemed a smart and safe idea to put to the challenge.

With a very seasoned hand on our intuitive and talented lead pony, we took her to bigger digs to begin jogging and galloping with a rider aboard. So much for human intellect. Like most Alphas, Jay was smart. She had been conditioned to understand that she was in charge where riding lessons were concerned and didn't take kindly to a new paradigm. For the first hour, she exhausted her load by refusing to go, trying to rub the rider off on the fence, and resisting the lead pony companion. Then, she launched into her bronc persona for what seemed like an eternity. While she failed to meet her expectations of a launch intended to set a new trajectory record, she was exhausting with her incredible athleticism that included not only putting the person on her back through the wringer but, also, unsettling the pony rider to the point where she turned Jay loose repeatedly. So, we chose to call it quits before the lesson should have been over, to save face and the likelihood of regression vs. a mere status quo. We ended without attaining a cooperative attitude, but also avoided broken bones. A win would have been better, but it was clear she was more fit and more determined than we were, at least on that particular day; so, we settled for a non-loss that included an ending note with the rider still seated safely aboard.

The call went out for reinforcements.

The next lesson was interesting and effective. We grabbed a couple of crazy brothers. Both were seasoned riders, and one was an incredible hand on a horse. These two were fearless in their youthful perspective — young and dumb helps sometimes with these types. They were forewarned about this filly's temperament and history. What they did was dangerous but effective. Halcyon Acres staff familiar with this filly started initial groundwork with full tack. Subsequently, we moved out of the round pen and into a one-acre paddock. The brothers then took over; one grabbed the end of a longe line in one hand with a twenty-foot whip in another, while we legged the other up onto Jay's back. Then, they drove her until she was compliant. The rider kicked her forward while the ground person kept the whip active at her haunches. The ground person restricted her ability to gain her balance during rider launch attempts by controlling her head, and consequently her balance, with the line. The whip and leg were ever present, and Jay was concerned enough by these crazy brothers to move away from the stimuli instead of trying to wheel, buck hard enough for a rider flight over her head, or slam on the brakes with finesse. Every day they worked with her, she continued to protest but, ultimately, during each session she was tired and confused enough to be released from the longe line and behave when responding to unfettered rider cues. We ponied her on the trails for a couple of days with full tack (but no rider) prior to shipping her to the track.

The first day at the racetrack, we tacked her up, but put no rider on her, and headed to the main (vs. the smaller and more distant training track), where she willingly and impressively trained with a lead pony. Of course, nothing ever seemed to come without unexpected challenges where this filly was concerned, and so, not surprisingly, some tack adjustments were necessary for success. In this case, the lead rope was attached to the bit, which resulted in Jay, quite understandably, planting herself each time pressure was applied. Once the lead was moved to the halter, she proceeded happily like a seasoned pro. Issues had become the norm with Jay, though, and this was a minor one given the incredible forward strides accomplished in a matter of minutes. Using a lead pony without a rider astride introduced her to the surroundings in a manner she could easily accept and added the benefit of a horse companion. The next day, we put a rider on her, and she behaved admirably — alone. She had some subsequent issues at the track with riders (in the barn or leaving the barn), but only prior to reaching the track for training. Since we took every precaution to ensure time on the track was pleasant and cooperative, she quickly learned to relish the exercise regimen and handle all on-track activities with an attentive and cooperative attitude. Even gate work was a non-event for this previously cantankerous filly. Today, she easily and competently carries an exercise rider of any experience level with a willing and responsive demeanor. She has also proven herself a winner — defeating allowance company challengers on race day.

Could we have put tools such as hobbles, restrictive headgear, or painful gadgets to discourage bad behavior into the mix to immobilize this filly into quicker compliance? Probably, but breaking the spirit of the horse is rarely effective when your goal is a performance animal — and this is especially true with Alphas. You want to channel, not defeat, their penchant for winning. Physical domination tends to solve immediate challenges, but can destroy what makes Alphas so impressive when they are properly turned to become allies vs. adversaries. Focusing their will and athleticism on accomplishments that are rider driven can produce amazing results. Ultimately, these mounts are the best team players you'll ever encounter, provided you can transform them into achievers that respect you to the point where they share your goals. Together, you can excel to extraordinary accomplishments.

OVERWHELMED AND CAGEY

Rosie spent two days at the racetrack after being "broke" at a distant farm. She wheeled about thirty times in a single trip jogging around a half-mile training track, terrified of oncoming traffic and the scene that presented itself to this unprepared, frenzied baby. At Thoroughbred racetracks, generally jogging (or trotting) horses travel on the outside rail moving to the left; galloping horses and those moving at a faster pace track right toward the inside rail. On day two, in a half-mile gallop (we tried a different approach to the oncoming traffic concern and started tracking right), she slammed into the rail at least a dozen times and ran at full speed in a panic — sans steering or brakes — not seeing, hearing, or feeling anything in her path of sheer, all-out, running terror.

She was trucked to Halcyon Acres that week for some reprogramming authorized by a trainer in a huge hurry to get her back. He failed to recognize the increased challenges associated with retooling a horse that had been poorly started. Still, we were determined to help this filly cope with what would be ahead of her. Of course, the idea of the imminent broken human body parts that would result if she wasn't removed from the track for a more controlled turning process was a factor.

Since time was of the essence, we started her in the round pen the day she was trucked in. It's preferable to give young horses time to settle into a routine prior to tackling performance challenges, but, sometimes, you make less than ideal choices with the horse's ultimate welfare in mind. We began with a brief lesson in responding to body language and voice commands that set the tone for future success with a quick reward for responding to easy requests. She understood.

Day two was a lengthy session, as was the case for the term of her stay, struggling to encourage a filly who had apparently no good ground-handling experience to perform simple tasks like picking up her feet and accepting basic grooming. First, we spent more than an hour each day in the stall, tackling activities that most yearlings are prepared to easily tolerate. This was a filly that was expected to perform on cue with a rider atop at the track! No wonder she was unresponsive, as terror set in, to requests she was woefully unprepared for.

We proceeded to the round pen and then the trails for under-saddle activities with Gatsby as a constant companion and teacher. Generally, it's best to implement short sessions, quitting as soon as a win is achieved, but we had twelve days to get this filly ready to go back to a track with a trainer who wasn't likely to permit patient daily regimens. Plus, Rosie wasn't very cooperative and it often took more than an hour to achieve a proper response to a single request.

The trails were tough at first as Rosie had little confidence in her mount and seemed to have no confidence in herself. Gatsby helped lead the way through troubling areas and trotted at her heels the rest of the time, getting her accustomed to traffic and noise behind her.

Once this filly started getting confident, she got belligerent. It became obvious where the prior "breaking" had gone wrong. Clearly, she was punished when she was scared and rewarded for being obstinate. (This filly could rear and hang with the best of them.) So, she learned to not trust her rider when afraid, having such reactions reinforced with punishment. It was equally clear, though, that she had found rider intimidation effective when she tired of the lesson.

The third day on the trails involved a half-hour rearing session at the mouth of the path to the back acreage. This was not a fear reaction, as the prior two days were met without resistance. This was to test the rider's fortitude. It was also apparent this gal had some practice with this maneuver, as she was able to maintain balance, with a rider on her back, holding a position perpendicular to the ground for a good five to ten seconds at a rip.

It was tough to decipher fear from fractiousness with this filly, and we responded to this initial unexpected behavior with patience and acceptance. When the next few days netted similar behavior at the same spot, we realized our initial passive response was wrong, and her behavior would have been better met with resolve. Since the filly had shown only fear prior to this point, the misreading was understandable, but still costly. Now, her attitude had been fortified with some wins, and she violently objected to our altered state of insistence. The Alpha showed up in clear fashion for the first time at this training juncture. After a few days of her impressing us with her athleticism and tenacity at a spot she had claimed as her opportunity for insurgence, now a point of rider contention, she acquiesced and handled future lessons eagerly and cooperatively.

Rosie spent one of her last days at Halcyon on an hour-long trail ride with company. We also spent time prior to heading out on the trails in a large outdoor arena with our lead pony, Porky — coming at her, by her, and riding alongside her at various gaits to get her accustomed to the rigors she would face at the track. Company was the last step with this filly. Even though other horses had frightened her in the quick stint at the track, she was equally lacking in confidence involving both herself and the rider. Consequently, it was critical that she first learn to go it alone and succeed independently without being reliant on an equine companion. Using another horse to guide her would have not only been counterproductive in efforts to build her confidence, but it would have also taken her focus off the rider for direction, making her dependant on company for cues and future cooperation.

Once at the track, her belligerence surfaced several times, but the fear was gone; so, combating training issues became a relatively clear approach of calm insistence, albeit a huge effort in staying power.

Sometimes, it's tough to read a horse and know why they behave the way they do. Scared horses need a ton of patience and some inventive approaches to help them gain trust in you. Most importantly, you need to teach them to have confidence in themselves and their ability to tackle the challenges requested of them from a secure, correct, and assuring rider.

It is equally important to recognize when a scared horse becomes manipulative. In Nette's case (Chapter Three), this was a non-factor and slow, patient, and responsive handling was critical to her blossoming. She initially was rushed, overwhelmed, and punished, so her natural tendency was to explode after any instinctive, mild fear response. Rosie was scared, but crafty too. Her initial "breaking" was textbook and all wrong. Recognizing when her actions transitioned from fright to fight was essential in reshaping her behavior and helping her to not only gain confidence in, but also respect for, the rider.

Channeling Rosie's Alpha tendencies will prove to be far more important in the long run with this talented, willful filly than the work we did to build her confidence. She's no longer scared and any issues associated with related early problems have been addressed. Alphas are smart and retain lessons learned. Rosie certainly proved her tendencies here. Clearly, based on our experiences at the farm, she truly found her stride through prior rewards for intimidating tactics, and these wins shaped her subsequent approach to frustrations with her riders' stupidity. She will likely test all who dare to ride her but now understands how fun, rewarding, and invigorating it can be to carry a rider who strives toward a common and mutually agreed-upon winning goal.

Horse Sense with Alphas

• Make sure you have the time, and the stamina, to finish a lesson you start with an Alpha. Staying power is critical and if you quit before the horse responds appropriately to your request, you'll regret it the next day.

• Chose your battles – and make sure you pick one you can win. Start easy, if possible, to gain some early rapport.

• Generally, Alphas respond better to a single handler. If feasible, work alone with these horses (but make sure you have someone there or aware of your intended end time who will check on you if they don't get a call).

• Respect is key with Alphas. Consequently, you need to be fearless (or at least try) and insistent with everything you ask of them. Back down and you'll spend many more hours trying to get back to a former progress point than you imagine. Don't take on an issue you're not ready to finish.

• Alphas are generally incredibly smart and cagey. Get to know your horse so you can recognize when they are trying to con or manipulate you.

• Most Alphas are very athletic – their heart helps them exceed performance norms. This can make them challenging and dangerous but also makes them potentially outstanding competitors. Keep safety in mind as you engage them and expect the unexpected.

• Alphas will like you more if they can view you as an able leader rather than a friendly, accommodating pacifist. These horses appreciate someone who can provide clear and confident direction more than one who gives them what they demand. Stand your ground and you'll get a lot further toward building a future amazing partnership than if you back down when they resist.

• Lessons learned with Alphas are retained. This includes both successes and failures. You will rarely need to revisit an issue that has been resolved in a lesson. Conversely, if you give up, it can take weeks, or months, to correct a problem you have permitted.

• It's best to choose one single objective for the day when trying to turn Alphas gone wrong. Do not push your luck by putting too much pressure on them. When the horse does what you ask, quit.

• When Alphas turn (and it generally happens suddenly), you will know it. Once you gain their respect they become eager pleasers and willing partners. Enjoy the rapport you have created and make sure they know you appreciate this transformation.

Chapter Six

ENCOURAGING A
TIMID EQUINE

TIMID HORSES ARE VERY DIFFERENT than those that have been conditioned to be scared. Usually, they've been rushed and overwhelmed. Consequently, a timid horse is generally insecure about surroundings and new experiences but not terrified about how their handler or rider will react when the horse responds with a fearful instinct. While many of the strategies in dealing with a scared horse apply to the timid mount, the process for undoing the damage is often considerably easier and less time-consuming. It's critically important, however, not to reinforce the learned fright by overfacing these horses. Slow and patient introduction to lessons and challenges is essential, as is being able to read the horse's readiness to proceed, if your intent is to turn your mount into a reliable and confident steed.

EXORCIZING THE CRAZIES

Spook was a claimed four-year-old Thoroughbred filly immediately deemed crazy by the new trainer. We were told she had spent little training time on the track, instead logging most of her exercise days in the pool, presumably due to behavioral and resulting soundness problems. She was promptly sent to Halcyon Acres for some reprogramming to settle her mind and enhance her conditioning for sustained soundness. Obviously, the endgame was to improve her racing performance.

When Spook arrived, we discovered that the perceived crazies were merely an expression of her insecurity, likely exacerbated by fearful riders who bolstered her concerns. We were told later that exercise riders working for her former trainer were terrified of this gal, and proven right as her behavior deteriorated. Sometimes, it's amazing how much the humans handling a horse can unknowingly dictate the horse's attitudes and reactions.

As is the case with most tentative horses, this filly needed some basic groundwork to build her confidence and learn to trust people. We started in the round pen with tack for a day or two. She almost immediately relaxed and settled into a comfortable routine that asked no more of her than she was ready to handle. We were able to hop on her back pretty quickly. Of course, consistent focus on praising her for quiet and responsive reactions to our requests was an important step in gaining her trust and confidence. Once she was calmly walking the perimeter of the arena, stopping and proceeding to walk when asked, we brought her to the center of the round pen and lowered a stirrup to climb up on her back. Interestingly, after a couple of days of discouraging her penchant for ripping around the round pen's perimeter, while encouraging a calm and slow approach to training requests, Spook didn't blow when asked to stand and bear weight on a stirrup, likely for the first time in her life. (Few Thoroughbred racehorses ever learn to stand on their own and bear weight on their left side prior to a rider landing in the saddle as they are generally held by a handler who "legs up" a rider by tossing him into the saddle.) Still, we took our time and watched her eye, bellying over her first before slowly and gently swinging the right leg over her back, after ensuring she was relaxed and ready. The first two days under saddle were spent walking and stopping. Sessions lasted less than fifteen minutes.

Once we were convinced that this filly trusted her rider and was ready to proceed in a slow and composed manner, we hit the trails. The first few days, we only walked. Interestingly, she tackled challenging terrain and the steep hills with relish, gaining confidence from her rider and blossoming from the praise she received for handling requests boldly and artfully. Of course, Gatsby helped her tackle the goblins along the way by forging ahead to prove scary-looking objects wouldn't attack. It was critical to never react anxiously to her fear. She had already had enough of that. Instead, calm, patient, and insistent reactions to encourage her to proceed, while giving her time to assess and accept the sights and sounds that unnerved her, was a necessary approach.

In about a week's time, Spook was walking, jogging, and galloping the trails confidently, comfortably, and quietly. In fact, she had transformed from a frightened and explosive filly to an eager pleaser who anticipated training time as a great game and an exciting trip toward new surroundings and sights. The next three weeks were spent building her confidence, keeping things interesting by incorporating a variety of activities and trail destinations while using the varying slopes on the property to build her muscle strength and add flexibility and resilience to her tendons and ligaments. During this time, prior soundness issues disappeared.

We threw the trainer on Porky, our lead pony, to join us on an hour-long tour of the property less than a month after the filly's arrival. Our companion was awestruck by the transformation. Her relaxed behavior and confident demeanor made this filly a stranger to a woman who had resolved herself to the likelihood she would have to endure a nut for the duration of her racing career. Interestingly, even with the option of a seasoned equine to lead the way, Spook happily and proudly led, forging through woodland and obstacles she had never seen, proving her newfound courage and confidence. Of course, this was all done at the walk — a prior unavailable gait for this formerly anxious filly.

The slow, quiet work on the hills throughout the property not only fixed her head, but also helped provide a foundation for future soundness. She was trucked back to the racetrack and began a previously elusive winning career.

When dealing with a timid horse, the mere introduction of a patient, gutsy, and responsive handler can result in huge dividends. Simply being quiet, confident, and clear about requests and gracious with praise when they conquer a challenge can transform these animals from frightened and unpredictable mounts to courageous, steady, and determined pleasers. Of course, a frightened rider on a timid horse will likely exacerbate the horse's phobias, so if you can't be the rock when dealing with an insecure steed, get some help from someone who can.

HORSE SENSE FOR ENCOURAGING A TIMID EQUINE

• The round pen provides the close quarters to begin to develop a rapport and trust with a timid horse. Here, you can establish some basic body language cues supported with voice commands to present yourself as a confident, kind guide while you encourage and reward your steed to tackle future requests with courage. While many contemporary horsemanship methods advocate considerable training time in the round pen, we're not convinced this is a good approach, and have found it is not effective with timid horses. It's a good starting point for a few days to see and guide the horse, but not the best environment to bring a timid horse along. Exposing them to various concerns in differing environments with a steady and unflappable nature is more effective in helping these horses blossom.

• Timid horses tend to respond much better to praise than punishment. Most timid horses love a pat or an encouraging voice when they face and conquer a challenge. Conversely, a stern voice and/or training that incorporates stimuli designed to discourage behavior tends to make them more wary.

• Take your time with timid horses. Their condition is often the result of too much, too soon. It's important to gain their trust, and bolster their confidence, by encouraging them with your steadiness to tackle easy tasks they can understand and learn to enjoy.

• Make early lessons quick and easy for an immediate win. Timid horses blossom and excel after just a few sessions if they have a confident hand and are rewarded for their effort.

• Buddies can be a good tool for encouraging timid horses, but don't overdo it. While another horse can help avoid some challenges, it's equally important to establish a trust in the human handler to keep them out of harm's way. If all issues are resolved by another horse leading the way, the timid equine will not gain the confidence in themselves and their rider/handler to excel.

• Give timid horses the time to process a lesson. Rush them and they will become more concerned and less trusting of you.

• Be fearless with timid horses. They will sense your concern and react. If you can't be confident, patient and calm in all situations you introduce them to, find someone who can.

Chapter Seven

TURNING A SOUR MOUNT

THERE ARE A NUMBER OF circumstances that can make a mount sour. One who has been drilled too hard in the arena and given little opportunity to relax in different surroundings can often be transformed by backing off of the flatwork and jumping. Simply choosing a varied routine that gets them fit and supple on the trails or in other new and interesting environments can quickly improve your mount's attitude. If your horse is sore and hasn't been forced to the point of resenting the mere appearance of a rider, giving him time off to heal and adopting a subsequent sensitivity to their pain can work wonders. Some horses are inadvertently taught to refuse. If there's been a pattern of curtailing every lesson as soon as the horse starts acting surly toward requests, this behavior will escalate, and the horse will object more frequently and dramatically to even simple tasks. These equines can usually be corrected with the aid of a seasoned and clever trainer, but this will often require that you watch on the sidelines initially, proceeding with closely monitored riding lessons after the horse is sufficiently schooled to discourage this behavior.

If you're dealing with a horse that has learned to resent with a vengeance the competitive arena for which they were intended, however, it might be time to find another project. While turning these animals to a point where they get the job done is possible, they're generally not very much fun to work with or be around. Plus, their attitudes leave them performing short of their potential. If they've turned mean, they add a considerable degree of danger to the mix. Mean horses that have learned that violence and refusal is their only recourse for avoiding pain are almost impossible to completely turn. You can make a lot of progress with them and often diffuse much of the mean behavior, but if they are sour and have been taught that belligerence is their only relief, they may be tough to tackle.

With any sour horse, it's important to be creative and responsive in how you approach the training and communication regimen.

STUDLEY

All deemed Studley a lost cause, except his insightful, reticent trainer who wasn't ready to admit defeat with this horse and his green owners, who were enamored by the idea of having a racehorse stallion. The moment he arrived, we began to question our creative capabilities with this monster, not to mention our sanity. As noted earlier (see Chapter Six — Turning Mean to Green), he was a vicious stud who had a history of maiming the humans he encountered and a quarrelsome attitude that rendered training attempts at the track impossible. After we developed a strategy and system that, over time, was effective at dissipating the meanness, moving from a survival to a success focus to address his sour nature became a priority. Ultimately, it was clear we'd have to work around his bad attitude to get this beast fit enough for speed training.

Sometimes sour comes with mean, and you have to placate the horse's hate of humans before you can even begin to address the refusal issues. Usually, mean horses have been beaten into submission or forced to perform through extreme pain to a point where they find the only recourse is violence. This can create a dangerous horse, particularly if they are abused to the stage where their existing physical pain makes any additional hurt a person can put on them inconsequential. If they don't care anymore what you do to them, they quickly learn that they are bigger and stronger and can certainly be nastier — and more effective — than you on your worst day. It's critical with these angry equines to work toward an understanding that you can control them but will not do so through violence, no matter how much they bait you. Consequently, groundwork is essential in reshaping their attitudes and asserting your leadership qualities before you can ever hope to make gains on their backs.

With Studley, the longe whip proved the critical tool in saving our necks and beginning to direct his movement. We spent over a week merely standing our ground in the round pen — much of the time with him loose — simply requesting, then insisting, he walk in the direction we chose. His initial instinct was to attack and try to intimidate the handler. Interestingly, he showed a respect for the longe whip and the handler who didn't recoil from his athletic and brutal affronts, as well as a weird confusion as to how to deal with this device. This is something we didn't expect but certainly appreciated. We never touched him with the whip and imagined, if contact occurred, he probably would have come at us with the intent to kill and any progress would have been illusive. Through this daily routine where quitting required submission to easy requests, accompanied with some isolation techniques — leaving him alone in the barn while others were out or making him the sole horse enjoying turnout during the afternoon — he came to appreciate human contact. In fact, he grew fond of human companionship and attention, welcoming it as time passed. He finally understood, probably for the first time, but definitely something that had escaped him for a long time, that people need not be the enemy. The meanness was at least out of the fore, and now it was time to begin dealing with his sour tendencies, which became considerably more apparent once we hopped on his back and started asking him to respond to aids.

Round pen work was interesting with Studley. He was quite willing to allow a rider to stirrup up while he stood quietly, which was a surprise. He even responded positively to walk and stop requests on cue. Faster gaits were a little more challenging — sometimes he'd comply but was equally ready to resist. Still, we felt we had enough control to hit the trails. On the first day in the "wilderness" we made it about fifty yards from the round pen before he planted himself. This became a routine each day for the next month or two of our training regimen. We waited until he was ready to proceed on most days, and this was a sufficient win for him to comply with future requests. Of course, patience was the ideal, but frustration sometimes turned to stupidity, and while carrying a crop was essential for achieving any gait faster than the walk — and sometimes a halt — using it in any way other than a gentle tap on the shoulder was a mistake. We learned more about this stud's athleticism one day when pressed for time. We decided to try to "send" him forward with a swift and sharp lace with the crop behind the saddle. It took us almost an hour to correct this mistake and progress mere yards past his designated stop spot. Studley had learned that any violence bestowed on him necessarily begot a much more dramatic reaction to avoid pain and suffering. We knew better but succumbed to impatience, and paid for it.

It became obvious that Studley would always retain many of his sour tendencies. While gelding him may have dulled them quite a bit, this wasn't an option, and we had to deal with reality.

The next month or two of activities involved figuring out how to get the miles under him to leg and lung him up so that a prolonged period of fitness training at the track could be avoided.

Interestingly, we found him much more comfortable and cooperative with a repeated routine vs. a more dynamic and exciting workout. So, we spent each day covering the same ground that included a couple of rounds around our mile-and-a-quarter loop and a mile round-trip ride to this destination. Every day, we'd trek up the hill, at a walk initially until we hit the point in the trail where he was willing to trot, then down the slope to the designated field. If we asked him too soon to jog, he'd plant himself, and we'd spend a half hour asking and waiting for him to proceed. Every second turn around the field, he'd slam on the brakes prior to proceeding willingly into a gallop. His behavior was tough on the rider's back, but certainly predictable, and accepting his demands in exchange for compliance with our requests became a daily requirement to getting this stud ready to race.

He continued to be a nightmare when we hit the track, but he was trainable. If a groom led us twenty feet past the clocker's stand, he'd plant himself but ultimately proceed, particularly if a horse passed him and he had a hind end to focus on. Trying to get him onto the track alone or having him turned loose too close to the gap left him backing all the way back to the barn in a pretty quick and, sometimes, airborne manner. Once we got past the six-furlong gap, we were golden, until we turned around and had to pass the three-eighths pole, where he planted himself again and periodically flung himself off the track in an effort to head toward home. Once past the quarter-mile pole, he was happy to gallop at a decent pace, provided you didn't try to rate him, and if so, he'd proceed at a blistering clip. That was Studley. We couldn't work him from the pole, but discovered he'd breeze willingly and artfully from the gate with company, so that's how we got him fit to run. His meanness didn't resurface, but all who were involved in his handling or riding were warned that any aggressive action toward him would likely lead to regret. He ran second in each of his five allowance races during the latter part of the season, and headed south to Florida for the winter with a younger trainer, a different set of grooms, and a new exercise rider.

He was barred from training at that racetrack in a month's time. He unseated the appointed new rider and tried to kill him (likely due to some aggressive handling by his new grooms – Studley didn't need a direct correlation to his victim after being treated badly). The jockey accepting the task of exercising him in Florida had the talent to ride this horse, watched Studley train in New York, understood his peculiarities, witnessed his athleticism with a deep respect for his ability, and recognized the danger of pushing him too hard. It wasn't over yet, though, because the resident cowboy, a highly respected, talented, and fearless track exercise rider, witnessed the incident and offered to take Studley on. The next day, Studley was given his walking papers. His meanness returned and his behavior was dangerous enough that it resulted in a track ruling to bar Studley from training and this game rider to admit defeat. Studley never returned to the Northeast to run.

A sour horse gone mean is tough to turn. If you're going to take one of these critters on, be ready for a long and frustrating process and the possibility you may get past the meanness, but will likely never fully eliminate their sour attitude. Before you embark on such a journey, think hard about what you want to accomplish and why. Does the horse have the potential to go where you want to get him if you are completely successful? If not, consider an easier and more receptive project.

Horse Sense for Sour Equines

• Rule out physical issues that may be causing pain and the horse's associated frustration in his failure to communicate.

• Do not continue to push a sore horse, or you will only make him sourer and could turn him mean. Give him the help and the time required to heal prior to resuming training.

• Figure out whether routine or varied activities are the preference of your sour horse and give him what makes him happiest.

• Be patient, flexible, and accommodating with a sour horse when their behavior is justified. Conversely, if you've taught a horse to be sour by rewarding bad behavior, resolve to stop the pattern or get some help.

• Try getting a horse out of the routine with some fun activities, trail rides, and long walks if his sour behavior is likely due to too much of the same grind. Some sour horses will bounce back pretty quickly once relieved of the drill that has made them bored and cranky.

• It is rarely effective to discipline a sour horse for his behavior. If a horse has come to resent riding, punishing them aboard only reinforces this conviction. Instead, try finding an easy activity they enjoy and rewarding them for their cooperation. Once you've gained a rapport, reintroduce them to the discipline training in lighter doses and with greater rewards for their achievements.

• Horses that have turned sour rarely become standout competitors (unless you change their career to something they learn to enjoy), nor fun pleasure horses. If your aim is to put them back into the routine that created their sour nature (unless this is due to pain you address and correct), you are likely to be disappointed. Consider a different project.

• Find some riding activity that's really fun for your sour horse and reward him with this after every positive response to a lesson (this could be trail riding, jumping, riding with a companion horse, going fast, going slow, a long rein, a swim in a pond – each horse is different and you need to figure out what makes your horse happiest).

• Know when to call it quits. Sour horses are some of the toughest to turn and sometimes there is no reward for the effort. If you come to hate riding or working with this horse, it may be time to say goodbye. Quality of life (yours and theirs) is something worth considering with these projects.

Chapter Eight

SOMETIMES THEY'RE
JUST PLAIN CRAZY

ON OCCASION, YOU REALLY DO find yourself burdened with a nut. While preliminary bad breaking definitely exacerbates problems, when you strip it all down and finally get past the baggage, there are times you must admit that the horse you're working with is simply just not right in the head. Interestingly, these critters can be very predictable in what sets them off, but how they react is never a given. Surprisingly, they can usually handle distractions and circumstances that should make a sane horse blow, but freak out with stuff that shouldn't be a concern.

Crazy horses rarely give you an opportunity to completely relax. There will always be issues that make them occasionally frustrating and often dangerous. Horses that are totally governed by fear rarely consider their own welfare when reacting, and this is a common trait of equines who are nuts. Mean horses are always limited with what they will do by a self-preservation instinct, making them at least predictable in how far they will go. Not so with crazy horses. They'll crash through fences, impale themselves, flip, run off on unsafe ground, and have occasions when they go deaf, blind, and oblivious to immovable objects that cross their panicked path, while reacting to ghosts in ways that make no sense. Sometimes, you'll encounter a psycho that has so much talent it seems worth the effort. Usually, it isn't. Still, we've had some success with crazies, and some failures too. Most, ultimately, leave you shaking your head on the time and money spent to get them two strides forward and ten steps back, wondering if the sanity issue extends beyond your equine's behavior and if there's a white jacket in your size.

While it seems prudent to try to recover your investment, sometimes it's best to cut your losses. Time and money gone is just plain lost — and putting good money after bad is rarely a good idea. If you're determined to proceed, the anecdotes below may help guide you in your quest.

FLASH — HURDLER EXTRAORDINAIRE

Flash was a narrow, five-year-old, 15.1-hand Thoroughbred that somehow wound up as a lesson horse at an area riding stable. He was a terror with students, running off at will and occasionally unseating the brave kids who dared to try to conquer him. One of our former riding instructors asked us to take a look at this horse. She was considering buying him. He was deemed unsuitable as a lesson horse (imagine that) and was on the block. We hopped on him in the arena, and after a brief flatwork primer, pointed him at a 2'6" line (there was something about this horse that squealed natural talent over fences). He cleared the fences easily, correctly, and with a ton of finesse. He had never jumped. We leapt off immediately and said "buy him." She didn't, and we landed the prize for $500.

The next three years netted unimaginable nightmares. We figured he had just been mishandled, poorly started, and conditioned to react inappropriately. Certainly, with patient and skilled guidance, he'd transform into a cooperative steed. We were wrong.

We'd spend minutes or hours working with this horse one day, progressing to a new understanding, only to find those lessons not only lost but problems magnified by the next day. Compounding the frustration was the fact that this horse would willingly clear jumps of any size placed before him, but was out of control after hurdling the fence, not to mention during flat exercises. We progressed to the point where we were competing in events, and if we didn't get eliminated in dressage (this was a common occurrence — he had no qualms about hopping over the arena perimeter, particularly when the judges used a horse trailer for shelter), we were sure to go clean during cross-country and stadium, almost always finishing in the ribbons. Consequently, we were thrilled if we were able to complete the first phase. We were also convinced his incredible talent over fences made it worth the temporary embarrassment and extreme frustration borne while we worked through his issues.

We spent a ton of time working with easy tasks that were met some days with understanding and compliance and other days with insanity that redefined the term "lack of control." There was little need for over-fences training as he was a natural and jumping made him hotter, so most of our time was spent on minor restraint issues on the flat. When Flash decided to run off, there was no stopping him and no productive way to finish a lesson designed to instill control. When he was not right in the head, you simply couldn't get through to him — no matter how creative or excruciating the approach. Any lesson that descended into a situation that required a correction meant frustrating, subsequent weeks of simply striving to get back the progress we had lost. He was a tough case that had a ton of latent talent, but we found no means to extract it on a consistent basis. Changing to a stronger bit made him completely impervious to any hand aids. You couldn't get this horse tired. He was unable — or unwilling — to apply lessons learned on the ground to under-saddle activities. We had days where all we strived for was walk-halt-walk and failed even to achieve that goal. Other days, he'd perform like a champ, until his screw came loose and he regressed to his crazy, unreachable demeanor. We tried both short lessons and exhaustive, hours-long sessions in a mere attempt for a minor transition, but neither worked consistently. When he was right, he was a dream, but most of the time he was unstable; and even when things were going well, there was the likelihood he would blow for no reason, with his mind leaving the planet to somewhere way out in space.

It got so the prospect of even hopping on Flash for an intended fifteen-minute session, which could turn into a three-hour ordeal, became such an odious activity, his talent wasn't worth the cost. We decided to search for a new home for this gifted steed with someone who had a higher frustration threshold. We had made a lot of progress in three years and figured someone with a fresh perspective on this horse could bring him to levels of accomplishment that we were too tired to pursue. Of course, we also recognized it was critical that the new handlers understood the idiosyncrasies of this horse, and we were adamant about providing details to save another from the mistakes we had made.

We found a trainer in Connecticut who offered $2,500 for Flash, sight unseen (a steal for a hack in this community, let alone an accomplished competitor). We were adamant about his being unsuitable for the show ring (this was a hunter/jumper trainer) but expressed our conviction that this horse could be guided to a successful eventing career. Flash had already proven himself as unflappable in the cross-country and stadium phases, but definitely required some work in completing the dressage requirements. The trainer assured us he had appropriate students and would find a suitable home. We spent the money to truck him 350 miles with the expectation of a check upon arrival. He wanted to see the horse perform under saddle once we arrived, and Flash proceeded to run off (something we had forewarned him about prior to trekking across state lines). Of course, he also easily cleared several five-foot fences from a trot, but the trainer indicated, given his unruliness, he wanted to rescind his cash offer and take the horse on consignment. When we cautioned him that any kind of correction with either tack or brutality would not only be ineffective but also completely counterproductive, he looked our gal rider up and down as if to say "my six-foot frame and manliness is no match for your weak, womanly demeanor." We knew trouble was imminent. Six months later, we called inquiring about our check. He used some four-letter words to describe Flash and told us to come get him. Clearly, he hadn't heeded our warning and chose to try to fight with this horse. We declined the mandate to come pick him up as it was clear the "respite" from our farm likely involved six months of trying to bully this horse, a training approach that would probably require another decade of work to get him back to square one. Too bad; the horse had tons of talent, but was crazy enough to make anyone let frustration get the better of him. Sadly, we had had enough. Sometimes, you need to walk away from a problem mount that doesn't seem to want to work with you and appreciate the newfound quality of life obtained from investing valuable time in more reachable horses.

RED

Red came to us after having been "broke" by a girl who had little experience and less heart. She gave up after this four-year-old filly began flipping immediately following her hopping in the saddle. Apparently this went on for awhile, and this steed learned she could immediately and successfully end the lesson with this strategy. We spent some time on the ground with Red, as it was apparent she needed some preliminary guidance that had been skipped. We also wanted to establish communication benchmarks. She was actually responsive and compliant when we proceeded to under-saddle lessons in the round pen. Once we moved out of the confines and routine of this space, however, the flipping penchant resurfaced. In this case, we were able to step off as she went past perpendicular and hop back into the saddle while she was still on the ground, staying with her as she returned to her feet. That was the last time she flipped.

We had another week or so of good progress with this filly before her behavior deteriorated, and this time, she decided to lay down after we stirruped up. She was flat out on the ground and wouldn't move. We sat on her neck (this is usually referred to as sitting on their heads, but that's not really where you want to put your weight - horses cannot get up without their head and neck to use for momentum and the back of the neck is the safest place to be for both you and your horse) to immobilize her with a strategy designed to discourage this behavior in the future. Horses tend to panic when they can't get up and trapping an intentional flipper immediately generally teaches these horses to never go there again. She didn't care. Red lay there, on the ground, perfectly content being stuck. This was a first. There was something really wrong with this filly. We didn't have enough information to determine if there was some major underlying physical problem that was causing this behavior (she traveled sound and seemed to be unencumbered by pain, but we didn't dig too deep) or if she just had a major screw loose. Either way, this was one of the few we quickly determined was best to toss back. We called the owners and admitted defeat. They decided to forgo any future starting attempts and bred her instead. We'll let someone else tackle that progeny beauty when it's time to start riding lessons.

STEPHIE

Stephie was a crazed two-year-old already training at the racetrack who had unsettled the resident game "cowboy" enough for him to swallow his pride and opt off riding the headcase again. His out-of-control behavior and athleticism could get any rider's adrenaline flowing and cause bouts of sanity doubts while atop this special mount. He was one of these horses where the more you messed with him, the crazier he got.

We spent a couple of months working on developing a communications strategy that offered some control for the rider while allowing that this reactionary horse required some pretty creative and gentle handling. It was obvious from the onset that he had a lot of talent. The issue was gaining enough control and rapport to be able to direct the talent in ways that didn't put horse and rider in peril. (He did tend to lose sight of the fact that his behavior could get him hurt, too.)

Stephie was agile — and nuts. Whether the crazies were bestowed at birth or during early handling sessions was tough to determine, but one thing was certain — there was no going back to a sound mind with this one. Given his breeding, it's likely his brains were a birthright.

We didn't have the luxury of working with him in a quiet farm environment, as the owner and trainer were not willing to consider such a course of action. So, we struggled to get through to him to gain control and a modicum of safety at the racetrack environs. This horse was terrified and talented. If his fear could be channeled and he could learn to respond to necessary cues, he had the potential to be a tough competitor. Some of his behavior could not be modified, but this was a racehorse, and the primary goal was to get him safe enough to make the trip around a one-mile loop.

Our first goal was to discourage the behavior that was causing so many riders to walk home brushing dirt off their backsides. Interestingly, this horse became more alarmed when flying solo — he really didn't want to be making decisions without a rider's help. The problem was he was so athletic and quick that, when fear ruled, he usually unseated a rider before he even knew what happened. So, we went to work on trying to help this horse gain some confidence. It was a long, slow process requiring incredible fortitude. Timing was important as a goal was to offer as few other distractions as possible during training so the horse could learn to listen to the rider — and look to him for assurance when terror prevailed. Slow paces and short lessons were the initial goal. Once he learned to handle the sights and sounds that surround a training regimen in small doses, we increased the time and the mileage — but kept him on the smaller training track during times when few horses were present. Eventually, he became predictable, albeit spooky and slippery at times. It wasn't until after he was walking and jogging in a controlled fashion that we proceeded to training that included the gallop.

Once Stephie turned around to gallop, he wanted to do so at an all-out rip. Next project — try to gain sufficient control to maintain soundness. This wasn't easy and required some compromise. He was panicked about anyone touching his mouth. So, we changed the bit to a much softer model and adopted an approach that involved as little contact as possible — only half-halting when a modified pace was necessary, and limiting this initially to urgent matters (pending collisions). Eventually, he learned to respond to half-halts to modify his pace — although this cue was used sparingly. While he never got to the point where he could handle continued or firm contact with the bit, he did manage to tolerate light cues that permitted steering and some pace control.

This was a horse we made sure to introduce to everything he might possibly face on race day prior to his running, because any new stimuli sent him into a frenzy. Of course, it was necessary to ensure only one new item was presented at a time because his brain could only handle so much.

His first three races were interesting. The jockey decided to try to rate him. Big mistake. In all three cases, he bolted around traffic in front of him and charged on the outside rail toward the finish line — earning second-place money each time. Finally, the jockey learned, and Stephie actually wound up breaking his maiden (winning his first race) as a two-year-old — against allowance company at Belmont.

HORSE SENSE WHEN DEALING WITH THE CRAZED

• Be fearless. These characters can be dangerous and unpredictable.

• Get creative. Crazy horses tend to easily handle the tough stuff and panic over issues that are silly. Try and figure out what sets them off and be ready for the blow – or better yet – avoid such situations.

• Develop a customized communications process that gets the job done, albeit with less finesse than you would like.

• Be safe. Crazy horses are dangerous and unpredictable. Wear a helmet at all times and try to ensure you don't put yourself in dangerous territory or terrain with these horses.

• Be intuitive. Sometimes crazy horses have talent that can be channeled, but not with an ordinary approach. If you can figure out ways to communicate that may not be typical, but are effective, occasionally you can gain unexpected ground.

• Crazy horses usually require riders that aren't quite right in the head to tackle the challenges. If you view yourself as a little off, you might find yourself a fit for a crazy horse project. Sane riders best avoid this equine challenge.

Chapter Nine

CORRECTING COORDINATION
AND OTHER HEADACHES

SOMETIMES A HORSE SIMPLY CAN'T do what we ask of them — due to conformation, suitability, soundness, or athletic issues. Often, though, such challenges can be traced back to the starting process and corrected. Some horses need to be taught how to carry themselves correctly. Often, this requires starting the horse under saddle all over again. Others have just figured out how to buffalo their listening-impaired riders.

It is amazing how many horses being delivered, or sold, as "broke" lack very basic flat work. Riders who inherit these steeds (or have paid for a service that considers a horse that doesn't buck a rider off as finished) will need to address these missing training links if they ever expect their horse to excel in their chosen activity. This isn't rocket science, but does require paying attention to what your horse is telling you, taking the necessary time, and summoning the patience to understand and address these holes.

When starting any horse under saddle (or fixing a horse that has failed to understand or respond to what is being requested), an early aim should be recognizing and establishing rhythm. Anyone who has ever taken a riding lesson has likely, at some point, been told to breathe. Horses feel our tension and anything done on their backs to impede rhythm hinders performance. Holding our breath or shallow gasps is a natural reaction to anxiety, concern, excitement, or new experiences, but it undermines free-flow movement for the horse. When one takes a deep breath while mounted, both the rider and any observer can see the horse's carriage, movement, attitude, and posture transform immediately. Rhythm is what all other equine performance accomplishments are built on. Think of rhythm as the beat of a drum, the metronome in your mind, the steady hoofbeat underneath you as you extend or shorten a stride, the posting in the saddle that you do to keep your horse steady, whether going uphill or down. If you don't develop a sense for what is a natural and comfortable norm for your horse and learn to support and encourage this early, future requests for more demanding tasks will be a problem. Whether your aim is to safely traverse a hill on a trail ride, smartly clear a line of fences, excel in the dressage arena, or just have fun at home, your horse will not be comfortable if you don't address his need for you to understand, encourage, and support his rhythm. From this develops cadence, balance, transitions, security, quick responses to rider cues, and safety when confronted with difficult or new challenges.

Many riders rely too heavily on the hands. Any horse expected to respond effectively to aids needs to be schooled with leg and seat as primary drivers, with reins as a way to underscore requests, but not as the sole cue. A rider committed to turning a horse must first understand that trying to control a horse with the bit alone is an act of folly. In fact, if you pay attention, you'll find in most circumstances, your horse slows or stops when you release the reins. Learn to feel your horse with your seat and encourage him forward with a rewarding leg (that offers a release for responding by immediately easing the pressure). It's tough to feel a horse through rigid or unforgiving hands. Listening and asking with acute, soft and responsive aids will help you immensely as you strive to communicate with your mount.

If you don't know how to use your seat and leg to control the horse, you're losing seventy-five percent or more of your effectiveness on a horse. Consider finding someone who can help you understand how important these abilities are in communicating with your horse — and how to use them.

EVIL EARNED HIS NAME

Evil acquired his name the day he left the farm where he was born. The loading ordeal that transpired when his intended first mounts showed up to pick him up earned him the moniker. His subsequent behavior made the initial characterization tame. They responded to his viciousness in kind and felt accomplished in bringing a horse to the track that would carry a rider without trying to dump him. But dump him he did. He was so heavy on the forehand that he continually stumbled and somersaulted on occasion — sending both rider and horse to an unceremonious dump in the dirt.

He showed up at Halcyon Acres the next year with the "evil" warning and the conviction that trying to fix his stumbling was an inanity. Still, the owners bred this horse and felt compelled to try one last time to make him useful.

Evil showed his colors almost immediately — as soon as he was asked to engage himself properly. We quickly learned that, surprisingly, he was extremely lazy. We also realized that he didn't understand how to carry a rider comfortably, maintain a consistent pace or stride at any gait, nor balance himself to handle transitions or slight hills without falling apart.

He needed to learn to cooperate if we hoped to fix his performance issues. Perhaps, more importantly, though, he needed a basic education on how to hold it together with a rider on his back. While Evil was mad about being asked to work, he was equally frustrated with his inability to stay steady under saddle.

We spent a good two weeks dealing with refusals and violent responses in sessions where we insisted on a positive endnote. He kicked out, planted himself, tried to bite the rider, and showcased his launching techniques when asked for a simple 20-meter circle at the trot. As we continued to insist on proper impulsion and a correct bend, he became less cantankerous, but still wasn't very focused on cooperation. We spent some time working on rhythm and cadence with very slight inclines thrown into the mix, which Evil found extremely challenging. Once we were able to complete a circle with a stride that didn't quicken and shorten going downhill and slow on the uphill side, we moved to more interesting — and more challenging — environs. Basic dressage in a classic environment was a good start, but it wasn't going to ultimately get us where we needed to be in a reasonable amount of time.

At this juncture, we decided to hit the trails — which included some steep and hairy hills. This was done at the walk almost exclusively, initially. The first time we hit a good downhill slope we were ready to bail. He was so heavy on the forehand, a head-over-heels trip down the embankment seemed likely. Initially, he resisted rider aids to help him rock back on his haunches. Then he got it, and appreciated the help. Over time, he began to relish the trails and hills and became adept at handling any slope or sharp turn at the walk, trot, and even gallop. We spent a majority of the training time with this horse traveling through paths that traversed the woodlands, fields, orchards, water, and most significantly the hills indicative of the property landscape. His balance improved, his confidence soared, and he grew to appreciate the rides that offered the most challenging terrain. Over time, his mind understood the cues to help him stay safe, his body developed the necessary support system to carry out requested tasks, and his attitude blossomed, turning him into a willing and eager mount.

Evil became so comfortable and easygoing during his training exercises at the farm that he was used (with the owner's knowledge and blessing) as a lead pony toward the end of his stay. His transformation was incredible — and a source of pride for him, his owners, and the crew that got him there.

Prior to sending him back to the track, we did spend a good week with some dressage work in the arena to reinforce what he had already learned and to ensure prior problems would not likely resurface. His balance and carriage had improved to the point that he was able to perform some First Level Dressage tasks at various gaits when requested, easily and handily.

He went back to the track and into training as a safe steed. He made it to the races. He won, too. Evil never proved to be too talented as a racehorse but was sold as a capable and cooperative riding horse ready to carry a novice or more experienced mount willingly, safely, and intelligently.

Who's in charge?

It's not unusual to find a horse that's been started badly but figures it out despite the fact. It's also equally common to watch the same horse outsmart his teacher by feigning ignorance, confusion, concern, or consternation. Much of this is justified, and while corrections to the equine can be relatively easy, it's important to ensure the rider is brought into the mix for long-term solutions.

Putz

Ponies and kids don't always mix. Putz had been started under saddle by her owner — an eleven-year-old. The problem was, the more riding this young girl did, the more the horse refused to do what she asked. By the time Putz arrived at Halcyon Acres, this filly was responding to any riding equipment with pinned ears, a whipping tail, and bared teeth, ready to take some flesh with them. You could get on her. She'd stand for that — and then just stand. Ask her do something and the tail would get animated, the ears would lie flat, and she'd start grinding her teeth. Keep it up, and she'd be buckling at the knees and hocks in a crouch that threatened lying down, done more as an intimidation tactic than a move with intent.

It only took a couple of weeks to fix the problem — once we got the kid off her back and the horse away from home. That was the easy part. It was merely a matter of being persistent about insisting on responses. Simply asking, until she responded, and then releasing the pressure, was an effective approach with this crafty little steed. At times, she did get determined and violent in her objections — and those tantrums were met with a swift and meaningful correction that included a single sharp crack on her haunches with a crop, a boot in the ribs with the leg or, occasionally, a rap on the bars of the mouth when her front end was belligerent or unresponsive. She didn't like that, but understood exactly what she was being indicted with, and quickly decided it was far easier to relent. This was a smart pony that understood the requests — but had learned that it was more fun, and less work, to say no. Of course, there's no telling what the kid did to get her there, but it didn't take long to render a fix that was cool with the pony.

Anxious to get her back home, her owner took her off the farm to ride her in private. She was back in a matter of weeks complaining that her pony had stopped doing what she told her to do. After some lessons for the human part of the equation with her wise steed on the ready, the problems subsided.

TIPS FROM THE PROFESSIONAL TRENCHES

I HOPE YOU HAVE AS much fun reading this section as I did interviewing the professionals featured. Each brings their own perspectives and stories on handling challenging horses and troublesome issues, along with their ideas on how to make horsing around the best experience it can be. Granted, a standard format was the plan for these chapters, but our contributors had other ideas. Consequently, while the structure of each piece varies, the personalities and style of the highlighted equine communicator shines through, making the section more interesting and diverse than initially intended.

The honest, thoughtful, and revealing input from these successful professionals will help you gain different perspectives on how you might address a problem you are experiencing with your horse. My hearty thanks go out to the international mix of riders, trainers, and handlers who offered frank, insightful, and veteran comment.

Do recognize that these are professionals working with specific and sometimes dramatic problems. Each equine situation is different, and if you're concerned about handling a dangerous equine, or are not moving forward with your objectives as you try and implement these tips, consider getting some experienced help.

Enjoy the ride from others' viewpoints.

Chapter Ten

KELS BONHAM

Kels Bonham
Junior Rider and Grand Prix competitor
Savannah, Georgia, U.S.A.

KELS' PARENTS ARE BOTH HORSE trainers, so she was exposed to riding and competing at an early age. Her first A Circuit Show appearance was at the age of six. Since that time, she has competed with hunters/jumpers and in equitation classes. Her achievements include an individual win at the Medal finals as well as consistent performance at the High Junior Jumper and Grand Prix levels. Kels, at age 18, is now a freshman at Savannah College of Art and Design, where she's riding on the intercollegiate team.

WHAT PROBLEM?

"I haven't really considered any of the horses we've gotten to be a problem," Kels explains. "I've never had one that's been vicious, a terrible stopper, or hard to control. I might have had minor issues to address like sourness, or boredom where they do not want to do one particular thing like lead changes, but I don't think we've had one that's been that bad.

"I've learned a lot through making mistakes as far as bringing along a troubled or green horse. You need to be extremely patient. Anytime you try to rush things, something is going to go wrong with the horse's mental or physical health.

"If a horse is fighting you, it makes sense to step back and work with the horse. It can't always be your way. If you just fight them, you are not going to get anything accomplished."

PROJECT EARNS PRIDE

"I was very proud of a horse I had last year named Rebel's Run. When we got him, he had only done the baby green hunters, so he was jumping very low. I was the only one besides my brother that rode him; and we brought him all the way to the Junior Jumper and did the Medal finals. It was really rewarding to bring one along, and it made me realize how much I like bringing green horses up through the ranks.

"It was a gradual process with Rebel. When we got him, he knew the basics, but he was very green. Every day I made his routine a little more advanced — getting the steering better, learning to be collected, jumping more complicated gymnastics, etc. By the end he was jumping extremely complicated courses with ease.

"The first horse show I did with him was in Thermal, California. We took him out there to do the winter show circuit for six weeks. We started the first couple of weeks introducing him to the show grounds and courses, just not showing. When we did compete, we started in the very low jumpers with Level 1s, and by the end of it, he was doing Level 4. It was amazing how quickly he learned.

"That same year he was fifth at the six-year-old Jumper Championships. He did both Medal Finals that year. The next year, he started doing the High Junior Jumpers. This summer he placed in every Classic that I did with him."

KELS' IDEAS ON TRAINING

"Being on the show circuit, I've had the opportunity to watch a lot of people. Seeing their mistakes and seeing what people do well has been a great education. That's what I have to learn from, as well as my own experiences.

"I base riding and responding to a particular horse's needs all off of what I'm feeling. As far as starting young horses, I really like the (Buck) Brannaman system. A lot of horse breakers use the techniques he uses. You start them in the round pen, and it's all about getting them to trust you and making sure the horse knows you're not going to hurt or trick him."

Knowing your horse: "When you ride a horse, you feel if they favor one direction over another; if they resist certain things you do; even, to a degree, you can kind of feel what they think, and you have to use that to decide what you are going to do with a horse, and what it needs work on. It's important to get a feel for how sensitive a horse is. It's hard to get that feeling if you don't actually ride the horse. I don't think it works as well to train through a rider by just watching the horse and telling a rider what to do. It's much easier to know what's going on with a horse if you feel it firsthand."

Don't skip the flat work: "I think flat work is very important. A lot of people skip the flat work, and at times, I have been guilty of it. Many of the horses we got in labeled problem horses came around just by doing more flat work. This pretty much solved the problem without trying too much. You just have to go back to the basics sometimes."

Sour Horses: "We had a lot of horses come in that were just sour. They'd just be very grumpy about everything from tacking up, to riding, to behavior in their stall. I just really think giving the horses more attention really helps that. Not overworking them and making sure they get the things they need like turnout and grooming are important. A lot of people in the show world do not give much individual attention to horses and they're showing them all the time. Sometimes, the horses just get sick of it. Usually, if you're just giving them what they need, it keeps them from getting like that."

Keep your cool: "Learn that you cannot lose your temper and you have to think more about the horse than yourself when you are a horse trainer. Sometimes, you need to put other things aside for the good of the horse."

ABOUT KELS BONHAM

Kels is a gifted, mature, and insightful young lady. Even though she was competing at levels as a junior that many adults will never reach, she insisted on tacking her own horses at shows and connecting with the horses she rides through time spent on the ground between competitions. Kels has not only shined as a nationally acclaimed equitation rider but has also held her own in Jumper Classics against seasoned and celebrated adults.

While she admits she's not sure yet what she will do after college, she indicates she'd like to be a professional rider (some might argue she already is). She dreams of having her own small training farm where she starts young horses to bring them up through the ranks, with the ultimate aim of selling them to others.

Chapter Eleven

DENNY EMERSON

Denny Emerson
Olympic eventer, endurance rider, trainer,
instructor and gentleman
Vermont/North Carolina, U.S.A.

DENNY EMERSON IS THE ONLY rider to have ever won both a gold medal in eventing and a Tevis Cup buckle in endurance. In 2006, he was inducted into the United States Eventing Association (USEA) Hall of Fame. The Chronicle of the Horse (2000) cited him as one of the 50 most influential horsemen of the Twentieth Century. Today, he and his wife May run Tamarack Hill Farm, with facilities in Vermont and North Carolina.

MATURITY PROVIDES INSIGHT

"I think this is something that comes with getting older," Denny admits. "There are two ways of addressing 'my horse won't do what I want.' The mature, quiet, classical horseman will say, 'this horse won't do what I want, therefore, I am not asking him in a way he understands, or I'm overfacing him with tasks he's not emotionally prepared to handle.' But, the impatient person will say, 'this horse won't do what I want, therefore, the horse is being bad and I have permission to get on his case and punish him.' I am now 67 years old, and I need to figure out a quieter or more consistent way to ask him. If you could get the younger ones (riders) to have that more mature attitude toward the training principles, I think you'd have a lot less trouble with horses. If it doesn't happen in a week, or two weeks, or three months, then that's OK. But you don't start to ratchet up the intensity just because it isn't happening fast enough.

"One of the things that I really do believe is that there can be a very significant difference between someone who is primarily a competitor and someone who is primarily a trainer. Let's say you're going to a particular event in two weeks. Your goal is to win the horse trials. If your horse isn't going well then there's a funny psychological switch that says 'my horse is an impediment to my goal' and you tend to lose patience with your horse.

"If your primary role is a trainer, the objective is to have the horse go well. The event in two weeks is not the priority," Denny explains. Instead, he says a trainer's sights are set on finding the right time and place to ensure the horse is able to shine. Patient tolerance and an understanding of equine needs with a schedule designed for the highest-level performance is the focus. "There's a very different mindset," he asserts.

"The best horseman is the person that can do both — to be both is really good. I think it's better to be a good trainer than to be a good competitor. I've known a lot of really good competitors where others say 'that person can really ride, but God forbid that you be his young horse,' because he doesn't have the patience to create a young horse. They're too much in a hurry and they want what they want when they want it," he notes.

Denny indicates he's had his worst luck with horses that don't want to go, often horses that have learned to be sour mounts. He is convinced that many of these horses are reacting to too much pressure too soon, and he has had some limited success with trail riding such steeds with older horses. He lets them relax, enjoy the countryside, and realize that riding excursions need not be stressful.

He has had a lot more success with horses that are too eager or aggressive because, he notes, you can channel that energy. "You might not always have the most brilliant dressage test, but at least you can go cross country. I would much rather have a horse that's a little hot than one that digs its toes in." Denny admits he used to buy a lot of horses that were cheap, and the price came with a reason. Often it was because they were difficult, and frequently, that meant high-strung. Taking the time with these horses to let them get settled and encouraging calmness through long, slow trail rides with quiet equine companions has been a successful strategy for him.

Looking back — and forward

"One of the things that I've been thinking about is, you know the saying, 'I wish I had known then what I know now.' With horses, I think that if the rider is honest, and looks back over some of the horses from the past through the prism of later experiences, you would like to have another shot at that horse. You realize that you have made mistakes, that, with your new-found knowledge, you would do it differently.

"When I was starting out in the dark ages of the early sixties and right into the seventies, dressage almost didn't exist in the United States. There was a three-day team and a jumping team, originally in Gladstone. There were a few people that did dressage, but it didn't permeate the fabric of American riding. That really started in '76 when Hilda Gurney, Dorothy Morkis, and Edith Master won a bronze Olympic medal at Montreal. And, now, the USDF (United States Dressage Federation) is bigger than any other equine association. I think a lot of the dressage that I, and others, learned was not classical, but coercive rather than cooperative. I can think of any number of my prior horses that could have benefited because I now know the riding scale and understand some other basic classical Dressage precepts such as the idea that the horse has to be absent from tightness. These concepts apply to both the physical and emotional state of the horse. I used to have a somewhat adversarial relationship with some horses twenty, thirty, forty years ago, that I wouldn't have today. And, it wasn't their fault. It was my fault.

"And so, I think that some of what my generation had that was good is, we were able to get a lot of experience just out galloping around on our ponies bareback. We were able to fox hunt and ride in open areas. Those were some of the advantages. The disadvantage was that classical riding was pretty much unknown in the U.S. other than by a small group of people that were able to get access to the good instructors. I guess that is the sort of regret that I have, is that I wish I'd known a lot more about dressage much sooner. But, I don't regret the fact that I used to be able to hunt when I first graduated from college in 1963 and was able to ride in the Essex Fox Hound Point-to-Point race. Riding in the open was very, very natural. That was something you could do then. It is hard to do now. But, the educational aspects were not as strong, or as humane, or as systematic, or as correct as they are today."

CONTEMPORARY APPLICATIONS

Loftus Fox is Denny's current Preliminary eventing horse, and a standing stud at his farm. Denny indicates that he's been able to apply what he's learned from contemporary dressage knowledge by implementing gentler aids in his training to gain a softer and more responsive horse. This has resulted in reaching greater performance benchmarks for Loftus Fox, through a more cooperative approach to schooling. "Aids are nonverbal communications with horses — if you touch a horse on the flank with the feather end of your dressage whip, very often their flank will quiver, so you don't have to boot a horse to make it move over," Denny notes. "You have to explain to the horse that a light pressure means move over. Do a light squeeze and do it over and over again, and at some point he will get annoyed and move, and then, your aid softens. So, you're building a language. It never occurred to me in my earlier years, that it didn't have to be 'I have to kick this hard to elicit this response.' Quietly pester the horse, and he will eventually move away. What passed for dressage years ago very often created anxiety as a byproduct, which I think the more correct, classical system does not do. I wish I had known that and understood it. When I'm working with horses now, it initially takes longer, but then goes much faster, because the horses are more tranquil in the process. You don't trigger that emotional fight-or-flight response because you are using your aids much more quietly," Denny asserts.

TOMORROW'S RIDERS

"Kids growing up today may wish for a time, thirty, forty years ago, that they could be a little more of a cowboy — blessed with open land and a relaxed attitude toward risk, which our society does not now encourage. Litigation, safety mandates including helmet requirements, and predator concerns put a greater focus on danger and make it harder for kids and parents to just relax and let riding be fun. Getting further away from the agrarian economy and landscape toward a suburban environment makes risks the focus so it becomes an impediment to learning. It was a different era decades ago, and safer, because you didn't have all the felons out there. The population in 1950 was 100 million, and last year it hit 300 million. It was a lot easier for a kid to grow up wild and free in 1949 than in 2009. It's not the kids' fault. It's not that they are any less capable of becoming brave; it's just that the parameters are more pulled in than when I was a kid. That's a lot of what has been lost by this growth and all the attendant problems. A lot of it is fear.

"There's a great quote by H.L. Mencken: 'The one permanent emotion of the inferior man is fear — fear of the unknown, the complex, the inexplicable. What he wants beyond anything else is safety.' That, to me, is sort of what permeates the way parents raise their kids today, compared to how I was let to do my thing. I could ride up to Burnters, Massachusetts, alone — and my parents weren't worried because they knew I was on my pony. This makes you brave. My mother was a worrywart in general, but not about that kind of stuff.

"The demographic and psychographic forces that people grow up influenced by have a huge impact on everything you do, and riding is one of them. That is sad for the kids growing up today. A lot of the stuff that people used to take for granted is now so circumscribed and capsular you just can't do it."

PROBLEM ISSUES AND ADVICE

"One of the things that I think a lot of people don't use is long, boring, tiring — but tiring at slow paces — trail rides. I think with a horse that is aggressive and hot, to go fast with it is like throwing gasoline on the existing fire. We have a place in Vermont ... it's like sixteen miles and feels like it's uphill all the way out and uphill all the way back. You feel like at the end 'I don't want to pick up my feet anymore.' A lot of times, after several trips, hot horses are happy to walk and relax.

"Getting out in the open, letting them realize that an hour isn't a long time to be working, can make a big difference with a lot of horses. If I buy a horse off the track that tends to be aggressive and hot, I try to go with a horse or two that are quiet. You almost like to go out with a couple of Quarter Horses. And you just go for long trail rides. The problem with that is you need places where you can go do it, which a lot of suburban America doesn't provide any more."

About Denny Emerson

Denny is currently at his 48th consecutive year of competing at the Preliminary eventing level or higher. He has been honored with the USEA's Wofford Cup for lifetime service to eventing, the American Riding Instructor Certification Program (AR-ICP) Lifetime Achievement Award, and was inducted in 2006 into the USEA Hall of Fame. He's served as president (twice) of the USEA, was vice president of Eventing for seven years at the USET, served on the Executive Committee of the USEF, and functioned as Chairman of the Breeder's Committee of the AHSA.

In addition to his eventing career, Denny has been involved in numerous other horse sports during his 56 years of competing. He rode in his first one-hundred-mile trail ride at GMHA in 1956. Forty-eight years later, in 2004, Denny won a Tevis Cup buckle in endurance, for completing the 50th Anniversary of the Western States Trail Ride, the most famous and arduous 100-mile endurance race in the world. Denny has compiled 2,250 miles in American Endurance Ride Conference races, and was long listed for the 2005 USA East team for the North American Championships.

Two stallions currently stand at his farm(s), including Loftus Fox and Formula One.

Denny Emerson

http://www.tamarackhill.com
denny@tamarackhill.com

Chapter Twelve

JUTTA HEINSOHN

Jutta Heinsohn
Bereiter, F.N.
Licensed Professional Trainer
FEI Dressage Trainer and competitor
Ocala, Florida, U.S.A.

JUTTA HEINSOHN HAS ALWAYS HAD a penchant, and a talent, for dressage. She's classically trained, being one of the first women accepted into, and successfully completing, the then in-depth and thorough 3-year Bereiter training program recognized by the Fédération Nationale (F.N.) in Warendorf, Germany (1973). This was a very difficult program at the time because, formerly, it had been open only to men. Jutta also achieved landmark status when she competed the first warmbloods in Southern California. She not only trains and instructs, but also continues to compete horses belonging to others as well as her own Registered Irish Draught stud, KEC Double Diamond through FEI levels. She has thirty-seven years experience starting, training, retraining, and showing horses in a variety of disciplines and levels.

OSCAR PROVIDED A DIFFERENT CHALLENGE

"Sometimes, the horses you encounter deemed mean, crazy, or sour will not even come close to the challenges a horse with potential can present, even though it makes for less dramatic reading," Jutta notes.

"I will always remember the challenges I consciously took on with a young stud. He was purchased because there was something unique about the way he moved. I watched his videos over and over again in slow motion and saw that certain something that called out to me and wouldn't let go.

"When Oscar came to my barn, he was four. He had already been ridden for a year and had been jumping courses over four feet. He could jump nearly anything, had a good walk and a great uphill canter, and while he could jump the moon, he had no technique, no gears, no ability to rock back and turn, and no trot, unless you consider trotting in front and tripping behind acceptable.

"Here was a horse that presented me with more challenge and opportunity than most. Not because he was an exceptional athlete, or simply a horse that deserved the opportunity to become a solid citizen (a term I've coined for my more difficult subjects over the years), but rather, it was because his natural movement was 'disconnected' and yet his potential, once connected, could be awesome.

"Connection in the horse is vital for any movement, large or small, if the goal is good execution in ultimate harmony. One of the most common issues I see in horses today is disconnection. From back to front, the horse should look, and move, like one animal. Optimally, a fluidity of motion from back to front in a circular, or rounded, form with the energy pushing from behind, is what one should strive for.

"Oscar had three spectacular looking parts (front, middle, and rear); however, when in motion under saddle, he was often uncoordinated behind and very mincy (putting much more energy into up and down rather than forward movement) in the front. When loose, his parts worked better together than under saddle, and since he had no neurological issues, it was safe to assume he was disconnected.

"I went to work on his muscle groups first: stretching them, massaging them, and working on the longe with the bungee [see explanation of this device later in this chapter] to encourage him to reach down into the bridle and seek contact all the way through his back. Relaxation over the back, rhythm, and throughness (when the horse is giving in the jaw and the poll while engaging from behind) were, and still are, the first order of every day, whether working from the ground or under saddle. Without these building blocks, a horse cannot properly connect to the rider or himself.

"Once Oscar found his rhythm and truly relaxed, I began working on his connection under saddle. Connection to the bridle through the rider's seat and leg was the goal. Whether in or out of the arena, on the trail, or in the field, exercises such as leg yields, additional lateral and bilateral requests along with half-halts, serpentines, and varying circular movements were effective. For the latter, we'd start with large circles and spiral down to small ones, then back out to large ones, always taking care to push the horse into the outside rein from the inside leg, and maintaining a constant forward-feeling contact. Oscar began to respond. His obvious visual signs of disconnection, tripping, and mincy steps, gradually subsided.

"Encouraging the horse to become and stay connected is an enormous step forward for any horse and rider combination. How many horses have you seen ridden upside down, short in the neck, and crammed together? I can guarantee these horses will usually be weak in the loin and hind quarters; show more muscle on the underside of the neck; be poorly muscled over the spine; and, will likely exhibit pain or irregular steps that you just can't put your finger on. By working a horse up and over his back, a horse's steps become longer and easier. If you miss this step in your training, you will not truly succeed in your horse/rider goals, no matter what discipline or sport you are working toward.

"Adding inclines and subtle, uneven ground with the exercises began to make a difference in how and where Oscar put his feet. Incorporating ground cavalletti as well — solid and unmoving poles are essential as rolling poles can cause injury — encouraged him to look where his feet were being placed and further enforced his hind to front connection.

"This may seem very basic to the reader — and it is — but without the basics, and very solid ones at that, and without always coming back to those basics, you will create additional problems, rather than solve them.

"Half-halts and transitions were also a basic part of every workout, and as his connection improved, Oscar's responsiveness and his timing improved.

"Working on the basics with Oscar enabled him to not only be able to jump the moon, but also be able to beat the clock, every single time out. Oscar is a large and careful horse, and yet he can nick under the fastest time by being adjustable, turning in the air, taking the fences on angles, and landing with alacrity. His ability to collect and push off all comes from those first steps where he learned his own rhythm and became connected. Today, Oscar can piaffe and passage with the best of them, and he can still jump the moon.

"Take your time, do it right ... cut no corners! Listen and *hear* what your partner is saying, then put your basic training principles to work and reap the results. Not every horse that comes through your barn will be a success, but I believe you can increase the quality of life for *every* horse by incorporating the basic training principles above.

"As a side note: in my endeavor to truly connect this horse and to improve his trot over time, I nearly broke his walk, by making it very lateral. Once you break a walk it is extremely hard to get it back — just ask FEI riders whose horses' walks have been broken during the collection phase of their dressage training. All was not lost, but his walk was less than stellar for nearly a year. A price I would willingly pay again to be able to see the results from our work together. When Oscar's trot was confirmed, bilaterally equal and strong, the very same principles used to connect the horse were what reconnected his walk," Jutta explains.

Tips from the trenches

"It would be most honest of me to admit that I really don't know what it is that I do with a horse. I haven't analyzed it before. I have a solid foundation of basic techniques that follow a learned and prescribed training scale that I benefited from by working with outstanding horsemen in my formative years and going through my formal German Bereiter training. From that point, my own experiences have honed my craft over the many years I have trained. Each day offers additional material to learn — each horse a new opportunity to further my knowledge. I don't think I'll ever have 'it' mastered. All I can hope for is that my contributions to the horses I've worked with have made their journeys more rewarding," Jutta admits.

Keys to working with a challenging horse

"Above all else, listen! You have to go by feel and intuition. The horse will tell you what to do. Of course, there is one hard and fast rule: never get mad. You cannot get emotional about the horse and the situation or you will lose ground. Frustration will happen. What you do about the frustration will be the difference in your ultimate success.

"Even a professional is faced with situations that require trial and error. The difference between a professional and an amateur is normally the arsenal of information, experience, and techniques available to pull from. While many of the techniques are available to learn about in books, there is *no* substitute for application and practice ... trial and error ... you'll try a technique; it doesn't work, you try another.

"There are many artificial aids and devices available to a horseman or woman today, and I suppose if you are looking for shortcuts, or a faster road to conclusion, there are some that are quite useful. I strongly believe there is no substitution for solid knowledge and natural, or learned, abilities. This includes a balance of timing and strength, an ability to read the horse's body language, and the insight to respond quickly and appropriately enough to change the horse's path while always providing him the opportunity to make the right choice!

"A few artificial aids that I keep in my tack room include: a longe line, driving lines, whip, spurs, and a neck stretcher (bungee). The bungee is my choice for introducing the young or problem horse to the concept of contact. This device is very simple in design and is fitted to encourage a horse to reach into the bridle and accept contact on the mouth. This tool provides an ideal horse's mouth to rider's hand connection in a kinder and more consistent way than most people can simulate. The bungee flexes with the horse, offering a forward-feeling contact. For any readers who use resistance bands in your workouts, you will understand the general concept. Unlike the draw rein, it does not cause the horse to curl and back off of the contact completely, nor does it create an end point — rather an increase of tension to match the pressure from the horse which, once he releases, immediately softens," Jutta concludes.

About Jutta Heinsohn

While Jutta's dressage credentials place her in a highly respected group of trainers in the United States, she's spent the better part of her life using her expertise to retrain troubled horses, start young horses, and fix horses that have been damaged or misunderstood by others. Humbled often by the extraordinary reward that bringing a rehabilitated horse back into the competitive arena provides, Jutta continues her efforts on behalf of the horse and the rider who is eager to learn.

Jutta takes a balanced approach to the horse-rider collaboration and their respective needs. She works with individual horses and clients on their goals, striving to reach those aims in a harmonic partnership. This philosophy allows Jutta's clients — both horse and rider — to advance quickly and happily.

At the end of 2002, Jutta became a United States citizen. Along with the pride associated with this designation, it's also opened previously closed equine competitive doors that remained elusive in the prior century.

Jutta Heinsohn
Ocala, Florida

Stallion@adsagsona.com
http://www.adsagsona.com

(352) 598-2873

Chapter Thirteen

DENNIS AUSLAM

Dennis Auslam
Redwood Stables
Western riding and training professional,
horse and human communicator
Minnesota, U.S.A.

"The most miserable people and the most miserable horses that I've seen are people and horses without discipline or direction."

—Dennis Auslam

DENNIS HAS BEEN IN THE horse business for thirty years. He admits he's probably learned more in the last five or six years than in his first twenty-five, due in large part to a transformed state of mind, increased maturity, and additional experience. He was born and raised in Idaho and developed a passion for horse training at the tender age of eight. Redwood Stables started there and came with him when he moved to Minnesota. Dennis has won year-end championships in numerous rodeo associations and has successfully shown in AQHA (American Quarter Horse Association) and ABRA (American Barrel Racing Association) events. "It wasn't just about winning to me, though. It was the focus on horsemanship, the enjoyment, communication, and cooperation from the horse, without resorting to intimidation," Dennis admits.

"It's important to start to understand that what we do causes a lot of our own problems with these guys. The biggest thing is we try to drag them into our environment and our way of thinking, and they're not wired that way. Once you start to understand that, you're much more successful, because horses don't like gray area. They want to know exactly what the structure is, who's leading the pack, and what's expected of them," Dennis explains. "We are our own worst enemies."

In the past, many of the horses Dennis worked with came out of Montana and North Dakota, gathered from the ranges and untouched. Today, it involves much bigger projects that include horses where an owner and, sadly, sometimes a trainer have tried to start them under saddle and hit a wall that made them unable to finish the job. "I need to go back to the beginning and figure out where things went wrong," Dennis notes. "I run into that continually and it's maddening."

"I love my job. I love working with people. The majority of the people in this industry are in it for recreation. So, why not educate yourself and educate your horse to make that recreation as safe as you possibly can? Buy the appropriate horse. If you're just starting out, don't go buy a three-year-old, buy a twenty-year-old. People get hurt, and horse riding is a hazard as it is. The wrong combination just makes it a time bomb."

THIRD TRAINER PROVED THE CHARM WITH SADDLEBRED

Dennis talks about a long letter he received from a gentleman who had all but given up on his horse and subsequently concluded Dennis was a "gift from God."

"I had a Saddlebred that the owner had sent to other trainers for what I believe was a period of nine months between the two of them. He'd blow up under saddle and in the harness. He (the owner) had heard about me from the mounted police up in Minneapolis. We had to do a lot of undoing before we could start doing. I had him three months, and I don't know the trainers, but I do believe that they were pretty whip-happy. This is one issue we discovered that leads to a lot of other areas. This horse had learned to have no trust and a total lack of confidence with the people that worked with him. So, we had to deal with that and get the horse over his concerns. He wasn't a mean horse. He was a kind horse. But, whenever you got in the saddle or hooked him up in the harness, he couldn't hold it together. I started him just like I would a two-year-old. I think when they started him, they just got on and went, instead of giving him the basics, putting a good foundation on him. I started in the round pen to try to get some of the cobwebs out of his head. There were times when I didn't think it was going to work, and that's why I kept him three months. I knew this was this horse's last chance. As it ended up, I did take the horse back to the owner's property after he was finished with the fixing process, and I don't normally do that. I hauled the horse three hours north of me because I wanted to see the horse in his environment, and see what kind of rider and driver this guy was. I took him out and rode him at this guy's place and hooked him up in the harness. The horse used to run away with the harness. He'd grab the bit and run, and did the same thing in the saddle, although here he'd rear first, then grab the bit and run," Dennis explains.

The homestead test for both the horse and the rider demonstrated that what this horse had learned in the last three months could be transferred to the new facility and the intended future rider/driver.

"The horse is doing very well. The owner called me. He had gone on vacation for a couple of weeks. When he came back, the horse was fresh because he hadn't been worked during this time. The horse held it together on the first day. I think we got him over the hump. The horse was much happier, much more secure. I don't think that horses like falling apart any more than we want them to. If we don't give horses confidence, we set ourselves up for failure as well as them," Dennis asserts.

WISDOM GAINED THROUGH THE YEARS

When faced with a horse that has been started badly, Dennis states that you need to go back to ground zero and start over. "There's obviously going to be certain areas that you can expedite through; this is part of finding out how you need to spend your time. There is no set way to work with every horse, you need to take each one on an individual basis," he explains.

Working in the round pen: "What I want to do is put him back in that herd mentality and establish some ground rules. It doesn't necessarily have to be in a round pen, you can essentially do the same thing on a long line. The round pen is easier on the individual. When you do ten or twelve a day, jerking on the long line starts to wear on you. Get them to face up. You need to show some leadership and once you get them to face up, then you're starting to come to a happy understanding for both the horse and the handler."

On Horse Trainers: "Being a horse trainer, like having kids, doesn't require a license. Anyone can hang a shingle out and say they're a horse trainer. There are not a lot of very good ones, and that makes a bad name for the rest of us. I wind up fixing a lot of people's mistakes, but what really chaps my hide is when I get a trainer's mistake. I know probably a dozen good trainers and fifty who have no business doing it. In this business, a lot of times you can reeducate a woman, but you're going to have a hell of a time reeducating a man."

Desensitizing and confidence: "Before I ever go to tack, I'm a big advocate of not just desensitizing a horse, but building confidence in the horse. Everything that I do leads that horse to the next step. I'm pretty thorough when I do my desensitizing. I want to get control of their feet while I'm on the ground as well as their shoulder, rib cage, and hip, to get control and carry these lessons over when I get on their backs."

Horse Health: "It's important to make sure the horse is physically OK. I always pay attention to the possibility of a rib, vertebrae, or poll being out of alignment, check to see that teeth are good, rule out sand colic; it's important to eliminate all the physical issues so that all we have to deal with is mental concerns. I have an equine dentist and chiropractor in regularly. A lot of this stuff (the horse care and maintenance activities to ensure a healthy mount), I can do myself.

"I'm also a big advocate of making sure a horse has the proper nutrition, because that ties into his mental well-being."

Moving from groundwork to under-saddle reprogramming: "Once I feel I have sufficient control on the ground, we go to the saddle. By that time, theoretically, I've built a lot of trust in that horse and I haven't violated that trust. There should be a relationship already built at this point to move forward.

"I start off the same way on the back as on the ground, by moving the hips, shoulders, and ribcage to get a horse to soften laterally. I don't even worry about vertical motion until we have so much lateral control, it's easy for the horse. If you're not doing this properly with the young horses, say you work on lateral for two days, and then expect a horse to start cantering on the third day with a high level vertical request, you create issues.

The horse isn't even comfortable with you at a walk or trot and now you want him to pick up the pace?

"Horses, like kids, need to start at kindergarten. Especially those that have learned to have problems. There are certain areas where you'll be able to expedite, provided you do it competently, but the only way you can know where to spend your time to build a confident and disciplined animal is if you start from the beginning."

History lessons: Dennis feels it's extremely important when working with horses that have problems after being started under saddle, to see the tack that was used. He has the owner bring his saddle and bridle and ensures all fit properly prior to putting his own equipment on the horse. He rules out (or confirms) that a bad fit or bad bit may be causing the problem. "So many times, when a horse is acting up, people don't tend to educate, they go up on the bit, with a more severe approach such as a longer shank."

ABOUT DENNIS AUSLAM

Dennis believes a problem horse is a rare find, but people who create them abound. He works with horses, and people, to help all involved gain the self-assurance, understanding, trust, and skills to find a happy connection for both. He teaches clinics across the country. One of his most popular training events is a six-hour, twelve-person/horse session that is designed primarily for women 35 years of age and older. He works with both the riders and the horses to instill confidence and understanding. He also offers roping and cow-working clinics.

Redwood Stables is his home, his business, and his passion. Today, he's most excited about the Bureau of Land Management (BML) mustangs he's working with, including one mare in particular that he is trucking around the country to horse fairs and expos, participating in demos and trail challenges. He hopes to adopt her after the money contest in April at the Midwest Horse Fairs Extreme Mustang Makeover Competition. He plans on presenting this steed as his future signature horse. One of the aspects he's found most exciting about these mustangs is the fact that they have been untouched by human hands, so they are blank slates and eager, willing learners in his hands. Dennis dreams of a day when he can devote total time to these incredibly obliging horses.

Redwood Stables currently trains all breeds and works in most riding disciplines. The business takes pride in its attention to both horse and rider, ensuring a good fit, experience, and future for both the human and equine components of the partnership.

Dennis & Michelle Auslam
Redwood Stables

http://www.RedwoodStables.com
redwoodstables@mvtvwireless.com

cell: (507) 430-0342

Chapter Fourteen

CLAIRE HUNTER

Claire Hunter
Hunter/Jumper trainer,
young horse communicator
Ontario, Canada

CLAIRE HUNTER OWNS BRAECREST STABLES in Loretto, Ontario, Canada, where she offers services in starting and backing young horses, retraining problem horses, showing horses, and training in hunter and jumper disciplines.

CLAIRE'S REARING HANOVERIAN

"A beautiful 16.2-hand, seven-year-old Hanoverian mare came to Braecrest Stables last summer because she wasn't working out in her current situation," Claire explains. "She was purchased to be a dressage horse. The owner sent her to a program at another training facility that expected each horse to fit into the formula training program practiced. The regimen was very demanding, with a lot of pressure put on the horses, and few rewards to encourage cooperation. The mare shut down. She developed a rearing problem, and outright refused to move forward. This behavior became so dramatic that the trainer grew to fear her, was afraid to ride the horse, and forbid the owner from riding her, too.

"Not knowing what to do at this point, the owner decided that it was probably best to sell the mare. But how could she sell a horse that had been characterized as 'dangerous' and 'unrideable'? The trainer referred her to Braecrest Stables as a possible resource to help sell the mare. We have a reputation for dealing with young or troubled horses and also have experience in sales; and the trainer was aware of this. The owner came by for a tour of our facility, and decided to bring the mare into our program the following month.

"The mare arrived, and I decided to take on this project personally. I let her settle into the routine without any pressure of work or expectations. She was turned out in a 3-acre grass paddock all day long, with a couple other mares for company. She was fed as much hay as she wanted, and was on a suitable concentrate ration for her size, age, and workload.

"After about a week, we had our first session.

"I am a strong believer in long lining for every horse. In unbroken youngsters, it teaches them directional aides, as well as coping skills when faced with equipment and frightening circumstances they're not used to. Such a foundation helps horses learn to control their emotions and reactions so they are less likely to explode with a rider aboard.

"The lines around their hind end prepare them for rider leg aids and help them to accept future challenges or entanglements without panicking.

"For all horses, it can help strengthen transitions, develop balance, rhythm, and you can use it to take them through difficult or scary situations without risking the rider.

"For troubled horses, long lining can help get them through difficult and dangerous vices such as rearing, spooking, and spinning, as well as bucking.

"Long lining also allows the trainer to assess the horse from all angles and evaluate their soundness and way of going. It helps identify strengths and weaknesses, and you can push their buttons and put pressure on them without being at risk on their back, especially with troubled horses.

"The long lining session with the Hanoverian mare went very well. She had impulsion, softened at the poll, and was working in a lovely soft frame. This mare tracked up happily, had a very good attitude, and was willing toward the whole idea. I long lined her twice before I rode her for the first time.

"Our first under-saddle session was very interesting for me, and her too, I'm sure! I tacked her up with just my close-contact saddle, and a plain hunter-type bridle with a D-ring, sweet-iron, French link bit — no flash, no dropped noseband, and no martingale. Her owner thought this was crazy. I knew it was necessary. By listening to the story of the mare's behavior and learning about her personality in the week she had been here, I knew this needed to be the next step. I took her to the outdoor ring and climbed aboard. The mare stood like a statue. She tensed her back a little, raised her head and neck, and her ears came back to listen. She swished her tail. I sat there, with a loose contact on the reins, and no leg. The mare listened. Her ears twitched again, she dropped her head four inches or so, and then walked away from the block. We proceeded about twenty paces, and she parked herself again. The mare halted, raised her head and neck, and swished her tail. I knew she was waiting for me to put pressure on her — to land a spur in her sides, or smack her in the hind end with a dressage whip to move forward. I never gave her anything she was expecting me to do. She walked on another twenty paces, and we went through the same routine again. She walked on again, and this time I guided her outside of the sand ring. We made our way halfway around a twenty-acre hay field, and she repeated the test. I repeated my answer. She walked on. We went for a forty-five-minute hack, and once the mare stopped testing me in that manner, she trotted on her own, willingly. She really seemed to be enjoying herself.

"We spent the next month slowly rebuilding the pressure. She had to be able to handle leg and hand contact, and be willing to work when expected. Throughout the process, however, I was very conscious about 'pressure on, pressure off' and respected her body language as well.

"We started some over-fences work and continued with her flat schooling. Within four weeks, which involved four to five short sessions a week, the mare was schooling on the flat, doing flying changes, and jumping a small course happily and willingly.

"What exactly was the problem? The problem was the program and the trainer's lack of sensitivity to the mare. Mares are generally more difficult than geldings for emotional and hormonal reasons, and you can often get far more brilliant work out of them than a gelding. It is very important, however, to be sensitive to each horse's needs, abilities, and moods. The trainer was putting such a demanding pressure on the mare, with no relief. No reward. Anyone under constant pressure is going to lose it eventually. This mare couldn't cope with the constant pressure. Now this isn't discipline specific, I think it's just related to the personality of the trainer and, in this situation, clashing with the horse to the point they were going backwards quickly. I think a good trainer should be able to adapt to any kind of horse, and get the best out of each one, often asking for it in very different ways," Claire states.

PROBLEM ISSUES AND ADVICE

"It's so important to realize how horses react to pressure, and many equestrians fail to understand this," Claire explains. "Simply knowing when to release is crucial in working with a horse, and not understanding this concept can have disastrous consequences. This isn't an issue that novices alone face, some professionals struggle with this too.

"A classic example I see is people holding horses for the vet. They grab on tighter as the horse starts to pull. This only increases the horse's desire to pull against the lead and fight. If the horse relaxes, the tendency is to keep a grip instead of releasing and giving a reward for the good behavior. This transfers to everything you do with your horse, from riding to ground manners, to training, to trailer loading, and perhaps most overridingly, to how fast you push them," she cautions.

Claire notes that a horse's natural tendency is to push back against pressure. It's uncomfortable for them and they tend to move into it instinctively. So, anyone who wants a horse to respond to aids needs to recognize that the horse will only realize what you want — or accept your request willingly — if they are rewarded for doing what you've asked with an immediate release. As an example, she notes that many riders constantly 'nag' at their horse's sides with their leg to encourage them to go forward without a reward of removing the pressure once the horse responds. This only teaches them to be desensitized and ignore your leg. It puts too much pressure on the horse, which can sometimes lead to severe problem behaviors, including bucking, or rearing, or outright ignoring you completely and 'parking.' A light leg, and carrying a crop to back up your leg to prevent you from nagging, is much more effective and presents a happier experience for both horse and rider. The same holds true for training regimens. If too much is asked with little or no reward, even the most agreeable horse will begin to object, sometimes violently.

"It's important when a horse gets it right to leave him alone," Claire advises.

Quick Tools and Tips

Long lining: "Long lining is an amazing tool that I use with every horse that comes through my program."

Round pen: "I use a round pen occasionally when I have a horse come in that has respect issues and needs to learn about 'my space, your space' commands and demands."

Free Jumping: "I like to teach all young horses to free jump loose before jumping under saddle. This allows them to figure out their own balance and stride while jumping, before dealing with a rider's weight and balance."

Turnout and nutrition: "I am a strong believer in lots of turnout and a very good nutritional program. A happy, well-fed horse is much more willing to cooperate than a horse that is unhappy, hungry, or has excess energy."

Handling: "The people that handle the horses on a daily basis are incredibly important to the horses' overall happiness. If you have staff that are afraid of the horses, or are too aggressive with them, this can greatly affect their daily behavior, especially as young, impressionable horses.

"Herd mechanics are key as well. If you have a horse that is being a bully to humans, if you get them in the right group and have another alpha that can put him in his place, it can help with his training and overall confidence. You do have to be careful with this, as you certainly don't want any of the horses to get hurt either."

About Claire Hunter

Claire Hunter specializes in backing and starting young horses, and retraining problem horses. After working at other equine establishments, she recognized there was a need for a service to bridge the gap between breeders and the show ring. From there, Braecrest Stables was created. In 2002, Claire and her family relocated from Etobicoke to a farm just north of Palgrave. It began with an eight-stall barn and two paddocks and grew from there to include an indoor arena, outdoor sand ring, eleven paddocks, and stabling for twenty horses.

Claire is an active member of the Toronto North York Hunt Club, Canadian Equestrian Federation, the Ontario Equestrian Federation, and the Canadian Sport Horse Association. She spent two years at Openwood Farm backing and training Thoroughbred racehorses and field hunters prior to starting her own business, where she serves as owner and trainer at Braecrest Stables in Loretto, Ontario, Canada.

Claire also has experience in first aid and rehabilitation for horses after working at a small animal clinic and uses this knowledge to help problem-solve and address issues with the equines at her farm. "I've ridden horses since I was eight years old and was always attracted to the difficult, nervous, and scared ones, loving the rewards of seeing them turn around and enjoy their work. After two years backing and starting horses at Openwood, I realized my love for working with young horses, and that I seemed to have a real talent with the young horses in communications and developing their confidence."

Claire was a guest speaker at the Ontario Equestrian Federation Annual Conference in 2008, with a seminar entitled "You don't need to be a superstar to be a success."

Claire Hunter
Loretto, Ontario

http://www.braecreststables.com

(705) 435-0330

Chapter Fifteen

JOHN NEWBOROUGH

John Newborough
Classic horse trainer and judge,
breeder and patient breaker
Lincolnshire, United Kingdom

JOHN NEWBOROUGH HAS BEEN BREAKING and schooling horses for about sixty years. Today, he spends a lot of his time judging, some of his time breeding, and has limited his saddle training of late to his own horses. He and his wife Gina work together with young horses at their facility in Lincolnshire, UK.

"Ninety percent of the time, I think the problem horse becomes a problem because they were wrongly handled," explains John. "Sometimes, other physical problems — when a saddle doesn't fit, for example — contribute. But usually it's wrong handling, or wrong handling for the type of horse."

He notes the importance of ensuring horses are adequately and firmly taught to lead, have their feet picked, and are instilled with manners from a very early age. Then, the breaking process is considerably easier, on both the rider and the horse. "Day one really starts with handling the young foal; if a foal is handled, everything is easier. The horse learns to be confident. I also feel that many people nowadays treat their horses as a pet; but they're not a pet, they are big, strong animals."

When it comes to the actual breaking-in process, both John and Gina assert that the horse needs to be physically well. "It's wrong to try to handle a horse that's in a weak condition because he's thin, or has wintered badly," John explains. "The horse cannot be mentally and physically able to do what you are asking him to achieve. People who try to start a horse that is not in good condition often create problem horses," he asserts.

A BONE BREAKER

Most who have worked professionally with challenging horses have a story to tell about a charge to fix a horse that has hurt someone else who tried.

"A man asked me, would I break a horse for him. He was a very good man. We hunted together. He bred a lot of horses, and I thought, why would he want me to do it? We were very much younger then. We were in our forties. We were quite busy, and I said, 'I really can't.'

"The postman used to sit with us and have a cup of coffee on his rounds. He asked if we were breaking any horses and told us that he delivered mail to a lady that specializes in difficult horses. About a week later, he said the lady had an accident. The man who asked me to have the horse said, 'John, I'm in trouble. I sent him away, and he broke the lady's arm.' He offered to pay any dowry for me to take the horse. I rang the woman; and she said she was long reining him, and he ran backward and broke her forearm.

"I had a gal working at the farm do the groundwork. He was a pig of a horse. All of his life he'd got away with a lot of things. He'd get topside of the people. If he took exception to things, he would strike and come straight at you rolling like a bull.

"My wife has been riding all her life, and when she started working with him, if he came striking at her or attacking, she'd give him a smack on the nose with a longeing whip, and away he'd go. We drove him miles and miles. We did have a few battles, and sometimes he got away. We'd work with him two or three times a day. We got him used to a roll, and he wasn't too bad with tack. But, he was pretty talented with his heels and would kick like a mule.

"We had one space in a cattle shed with a lot of cattle. It was what we call in this country a cubical house. He was in one stall in a row of seventy-two cattle stalls in this shed. He had the cattle moving constantly around him. He was tied in this stall with a hay net. Every morning, I took the cattle dung out with a tractor and back-mounted scraper. Initially, he would kick at the tractor as I scraped muck out behind him, but he just became used to everything. As I went down with the scraper he'd respond with a bang! bang! I'd hear him kicking every time with the scraper. He became accustomed to it, because he eventually learned we weren't going to hurt him.

"I had tins with pebbles and a sack full of straw on a rope which hung down from the roof, so he got used to something constantly touching him. As he touched it, it would swing, and ultimately, he came to perfectly accept it. I'd stand up on the stall partitions and lean over him several times a day and rap him with the sack to get him used to it and ready for later lessons.

"We'd probably be about eight weeks with him, but when it came to riding him, he was a Christian. What I put it down to was patience and a lot of hard work."

PROBLEM ISSUES AND ADVICE

Buckers: John explains that buckers usually have problems in their backs that make them uncomfortable. Some buck out of freshness, which he terms naughty bucking. But most horses that are buckers have underlying physical problems or are afraid because the groundwork hasn't been done properly. He notes that today, people are more aware of issues, but this wasn't always the case.

Phobias: "We had a mare that was terrified of pigs. Sweat would roll over her, and she'd be black with sweat," John explains. He notes he had a neighbor with pigs and continued to ride her past them over and over again. "We'd have some battles, but it's no good hitting them, because then they associate the fear with extra pain. They're afraid already. If you have a problem and a horse doesn't want to go somewhere, that's where you're going. I think a lot of problems start when a horse doesn't want to go somewhere. Say it doesn't want to go through a big puddle. Some say a horse doesn't like water, so they avoid it. We seek out those things."

John explains how he will often put a sack full of straw in a pen with a horse between him and his feed source. While they may stand in a corner blowing and snorting initially, he says the horse's stomach always gets the better of him, and he eventually proceeds to the manger over the sack. This teaches the horse to accept scary obstacles and events without a dangerous reaction when the time comes for riding excursions.

"It's not magic," he notes. "I think it's just that a lot of young people are very, very good theoretically — a lot more than we had — but it comes down to stockmanship, really."

Nappy: "You have what we call in this country, nappy. A horse won't go out of the barn or anything. That can be a problem physically because it hurts somewhere, but it's often initial management. There are only a small percentage of horses that are difficult. I'm not talking Thoroughbreds — racehorses — but with ordinary horses, people pay attention to breeding and temperament. You do get the odd ones that are just temporarily difficult. If they ever got away with something as a young horse, say they didn't want to go out of the yard and get away with it (this can be a problem).

"I don't think my wife and I would ever ride a young horse off the barn with company."

He cites that many people always provide company for young horses, getting in front of them when they don't want to go somewhere or spurring them from behind. Such an approach can make horses nappy when they are finally asked to go it alone. John notes he lives in a rural area and does not have the traffic concerns others might, so he spends a lot of time with horses on the road, long reining first, then riding with only his handler or rider as a companion. He's never had a nappy horse.

Watch the elbows: John cautions that horses tend to be very sensitive in the elbow. This can be dangerous for an unsuspecting rider on a horse that has not been exposed to contact in this area. With some horses, though certainly not all, he'll use bags of straw or hanging irons on the saddle prior to riding. "A loose rider can be a signal for fireworks if he touches them behind the elbow. We try to iron all these things out before riding them."

Start right to avoid peril: The initial groundwork is far more important than the riding training for a young horse, John asserts. Long reining is a great tool that he says is the critical background for breaking a young horse.

John insists one make sure a horse is "happy in its mouth." Besides being soft, safe, and smart with acclimating a horse to a bit, he underscores the importance of ensuring teeth are in good shape and engaging a dentist to check a horse's teeth for problems before starting any training, or trying to fix problems that have already been created. He also notes that a correct fit on a bit is critical; it must be the right width so it's not pinching and set properly in the horse's mouth so he cannot get his tongue over the bit. The bit must be fitted and made to encourage the horse to salivate. He uses a bit with a key, or copper, in the middle so horses play with it with their tongue and salivate. Little details can make a big difference. In fact, he tells a story of his carelessness with a bit placed too low in a horse's mouth many years ago, during a long-reining session. He noticed when he got home that the horse had his tongue over the bit and admitted he had many associated problems with the horse after that — ones he had created. "You learn from your mistakes. Now, we always make sure the bit is rather higher than you would have with an older horse. And, of course, once it gets its tongue over the bit, you have no control over it."

General advice: Make sure the breaking tack you put on a horse isn't restrictive. Use longeing very sparingly as it puts too much unnatural stress on a young horse's body and isn't a very good teaching tool. It makes sense to use the longe with a wild horse, to teach voice commands or sometimes for a horse that is in tack for the first time, but use this tool with discretion. Voice commands can be taught with the long rein just as effectively, and it's a better way to move a horse along.

Watch a horse's ears. You'll see them moving back and forth when the horse is listening to you. Talking to horses keeps them cheery. Make sure your basic vocal commands are consistent. Horses need to be sound in mind and body to be receptive to your requests. Always finish on a good note.

Backing (as it pertains to getting on a horse's back) is a gradual process and John starts by standing on a mounting block level with the horse's shoulder after coming back from a long rein session. Each day, when he feels the horse is ready, he'll touch his intended mount's shoulders and back, or perhaps lean and put pressure with his hands on the horse's back, and gradually lie over him. This is a slow process over days, where he's constantly assessing the horse's reaction. John notes that if the horse is wild or nervous, he would never attempt to back him. First, he makes sure the horse is at ease with prior lessons, ensuring he's mentally ready for new requests.

"A lot of the problems happen when a horse doesn't understand what someone wants," John asserts. "I know it's easy to give a horse a whack when it's not doing something, say it's refusing because it keeps shying away from something that scares them, but a whip is adding to the fire. If he's doing it out of naughtiness, the whip is another aid; but don't abuse it. Just give a tap and say 'walk on' when riding for the first time."

ABOUT JOHN NEWBOROUGH

Horses have been a big part of John's life, from hunting when he was younger to breeding and a lot of judging now. He and his wife Gina spent many of their younger years breaking horses for others, but now focus mostly on their own stock, including one they started under saddle in the autumn of 2008. While the types of horses have varied from Thoroughbreds to Welsh Cobs, ponies, cart, and draft horses, their farm focuses on breeding sport horses now. Seven horses reside at their farm, including a warm blood riding horse filly, a purebred Irish Draught and a Sport Horse mare for breeding, two Irish Draught two-year-olds as well as two yearlings — an Irish Draught and a Sport Horse.

John and Gina Newborough
Moat Cottage, Gautby
Near Market Rasen Lincs LN8 5JP

011 44 1526 397153

Chapter Sixteen

KATHY O'NEAL

Kathy O'Neal
Lesson and training stable owner,
rider and trainer
New Mexico, U.S.A.

KATHY O'NEAL OWNS LIVERY TRAINING Stables, a training and lesson stable in Corrales, New Mexico. She works with hunter/jumpers as well as Western horses/riders. Students range in age from three to eighty-three years old.

HAFLINGER BROODMARE TURNED RIDING HORSE — AT AGE FOUR

Kathy describes how she landed this little 14-hand filly that thought she was huge, with an owner determined to share in the riding experience during corrective training time. The filly spent sixty days at another farm being broke using Parelli horsemanship precepts that included some trail riding. Prior to arriving at this stable, she was kicked out of a dressage barn (which she later preformed at) because she was deemed dangerous due to her penchant for striking (although it's likely her other antics also added to the barring decision). She trucked into Livery Training Stables, still obnoxious, but with a preliminary education that made her manageable.

"She'd let you sit on her, and never made me feel like she was going to buck me off, but her ground manners needed a lot of work, and she was quick to resort to herd behavior when she didn't want to do something," Kathy explains. After an initial lesson with the Parelli trainer, the owner conceded she was in an abusive relationship. This was a comment made by the trainer that hit home on how the horse had no qualms about beating her (the owner) up. "It's so true," Kathy asserts. "This horse still drags her around the barn because she doesn't put a chain over her nose or discipline her for bad behavior."

"This filly was absolutely rude, both on the ground and under saddle. I started riding her along with the owner, against my wishes. Her owner was as new as the horse to riding. She was so excited about having a new toy; she failed to recognize how dangerous this recipe could be. It was a little scary to start with, doing this training with the owner in tow. We started with only walk and trot under saddle and worked to help her learn some manners on the ground during the first two months. I didn't even try to canter during this time because she was unreliable as far as going in a straight line, being a very green horse. She had a very mare-ish attitude but seemed to enjoy the work, which is why we continued to proceed. Still, she'd always go back to testing, especially with the owner. She was basically a pushy mare who would body-slam you, try to bite you, and spend most of her waking hours involved in obnoxious behavior. From the start, the only time she threatened to strike at me was when I would reprimand her for biting. She was not going to be dominated. In some cases, definitely so with this mare, you need to have respect from the horse before they are able to learn anything from you. It's an ongoing process.

"Originally, I led her with a chain over her nose because, being a Haflinger, she had a very strong neck and would just drag me wherever she wanted to go. That was sort of drastic, but something I felt was a necessary training tool. We worked on stopping, backing, and turning by pushing her body away from me on the ground. Then, we worked under saddle on walking, trotting, side-passing, and doing forehand turns. Just some of the basic stuff I teach every horse. This also included the beginnings of a roll-back, movement off the leg, and being obedient toward requests. All of that came slowly because her first reaction to me was rebellious. She would kick at my leg or squeal at me like she might to a stable mate. I needed to teach her that certain behavior wasn't appropriate. She had to get tired most days. I think that's kind of important. When horses are rebellious, you need to make lessons simple so they can be successful, but it's up to the horse whether they make it easy or not," Kathy explains.

After about three months of training, she was able to go in a straight line and stop and back. This mare went to her first dressage show as an entry-level competitor at the walk and trot with her owner aboard. Both survived and came home with two third-place ribbons.

Two weeks later, Kathy rode the filly at a dressage clinic at a familiar facility — the one she left six months prior with encouragement and cheers. While this mare did show her rebellious attitude at this event once or twice, she was, for the most part, eager to participate in the learning experience. In fact, the team was invited back for the next two days, proving her previously deemed unruly nature was sufficiently in check.

"This mare continues to tell me no first, but now with much less drama," Kathy notes. "She is learning to trust me and learning that I will not back down. I'm not a very brave person anymore, after many years of being beaten up and injured by unruly horses, but she was willing enough to learn the information through a process that we both could accept. What she does now is something I call backtalk — she objects and resists sometimes, but certainly isn't trying to unload me. I believe her issues have more to do with how she was raised than her bloodlines.

"One of the hardest challenges with this horse was the owner's insistence on being a part of the game from the beginning. Generally, it's much more difficult with a green horse when they're getting input from two different riders because they don't get the consistency. I do try to encourage my clients to ride their horses when they are in training, which is unusual in this industry. But in this mare's case, it did make it tougher because we were trying to resolve established issues. My challenge is always to make the horse and rider work effectively together. With this particular mare, I prepare her for her owner by having a light ride on her before she (the owner) jumps aboard, and also try to ensure the mare has at least an hour turnout prior to a scheduled lesson. I believe a young horse needs recess before being asked to 'study.' Prior exercise is critical to ensure this mare behaves. Lessons with the owner are kept short. It's important to keep the lesson within the attention span of both the rider and horse so that both can be successful," Kathy asserts.

Training Tips

Teaching Patience: Kathy indicates she's had success with requiring young or disobedient horses to stand tied and tacked for an hour prior to a lesson or training session so they learn tolerance and to stand still without pawing. She notes this must be done in a safe manner so horses don't hurt themselves, but indicates she ties them short and doesn't see too many horses that have a propensity to pull back. According to Kathy, "They learn to be patient with a saddle on for a couple of hours a day, not just twenty minutes."

Defusing fear: Kathy notes she's been trying to "engage horses' brains more, lately" by doing something as simple as walking over poles, or by rubbing them with a sack full of noisy items. "This makes horses think twice about running when they face a new situation. Of course, the horse's first desire when they're scared is to run," she explains.

Reprimands: "If you do have to correct a horse, do it quickly. You can't just do it once; you need to educate them until the bad behavior stops. Praise is as important as the reprimand and repetition is key. All my school horses get a big pat on the neck and a carrot after they are ridden. Some just live for that little pat."

The Voice: "I use my voice a lot. Raising my voice can tell a horse to stop doing something because I have that relationship with them. I have used my voice in the process of correcting them and so now I don't have to be physical at all. Near or far, they hear me and understand what I am asking because they have experienced my cues with the voice commands. Some of the horses around here seem to know English. Be direct and have keywords like 'Quit!' and 'Hey!' and, of course, 'Good girl'."

Education: "I've had situations here that were interesting. For instance, there was one little horse that was a kid's horse. When we went to try him to purchase, he was wonderful. He proceeded to become a smarty-pants horse. One day, the kid got on him and the horse immediately went to buck him off, and was successful. I was pretty close by — bad news for horse. I grabbed the horse from the kid, who only had his pride hurt, thank goodness, got on him, and proceeded to discipline him and get him tired. I was telling him 'all you have to do is be a good boy and behave for one hour a day.' I believe that was a turning point in that horse's life. Who knows why, but it seems like that horse understood 'I just have to be good for an hour for the kid and then I can have a happy home.' The family still owns him, so apparently, this has been a lasting lesson."

Competing: "I've never been one to get the horse ready and saddled for students at shows or at home. That is part of developing a relationship with a horse, and I think that's very important. Being around them is clearly how you can get the best out of your horses because they know who you are, and that you care about them."

Correction: "I'm not opposed to putting a chain over a horse's nose. My lead ropes are long, so I can use them across the chest to make a point. I've been known to use a whip, especially for pawing. If a horse paws at the gate, she gets slapped across the legs for misbehaving. It's important to discipline a horse at the point of disobedience. For example, if a horse bites you, you need to get them across the muzzle rather than slapping another part of their body. If they're pawing, use the lead rope or whip across their forearm so they understand where the disobedience is happening."

Artificial Aids: "I like German martingales because you can allow an amateur to use it, too, and not fear they are going to do something wrong with it. I pretty much ride everything in spurs because I come from a horseshow background where the discipline is to the nth degree. Horses are expected to perform immediately and spurs put a finer tune on these horses. It's rare to have to actually use the spurs on a horse once he's been introduced to them. The spurs are always there, though, in case I need them."

ABOUT KATHY O'NEAL

Kathy has been the owner of and trainer at Livery Training Stable for thirty years. Here, she works with horses of any age to help them meet their full potential. She spends much of her time today teaching youths and amateurs and helping them to reach their goals, whether for national shows or enjoying a trail ride with their equine partner. The farm uses school horses to teach kids how to enjoy riding safely and successfully.

In addition, Kathy serves as a judge at area shows and provides clinics for the local community.

She continues to ride and has earned several reserve championships at national horse shows in the past five years.

Livery Training Stables specializes in creating all-around horses that can do English (including jumping), as well as Western, trail, and pattern classes. Kathy's students excel at showmanship, which requires considerable discipline between horse and handler in these in-hand classes.

When not riding or teaching, Kathy writes articles for local and regional magazines.

Kathy O'Neal
Livery Training Stables

Kathy@liverytraining.com
http://www.liverytraining.com

(505) 688-0221

Chapter Seventeen

MIKE BONHAM

Mike Bonham
Grand Prix Jumper trainer,
hunter trainer, horse broker
Omaha, Nebraska, U.S.A.

MIKE BONHAM COMES FROM A family — generations — of equine enthusiasts and professionals. His children are now carrying the torch. His daughter, Kels, had accumulated five Grand Prix Jumper championships by the time she was seventeen and won the Medal Finals this past year. Son Chester (now a sixteen-year-old), is starting to focus on the show ring. Mike's grandfather, Chester Bonham (his son's namesake), won at Madison Square Garden at the Jumper Championships. His great uncle, Max, was even more famous, celebrated in the early 1960s as Horseman of the Year by the American Horse Show Association. Max's wife, and Mike's great aunt, Nancy Bonham, received the same honor in the 1970s. Today, the business is still a family affair and focused on efforts to train, show, and market hunters and jumpers.

TACKLING PROBLEMS

"There is no magic bullet for a problem horse," Mike asserts. "We've certainly had our share of problem horses. It's a crap-shoot and you fix some and you don't fix others, but usually it's never one hundred percent. It's very hard once they get into set habits, especially if they are a little older. These are quality horses, but they have lost their heart, most of the time through nobody's fault. Some horses can go year after year and others wind up losing their confidence and then they don't want to play anymore. It goes back to the basic personality of the horses that dictates their success, along with how they are handled.

"We are always training. I don't care if they are eleven or five. When you get one that has a general personality problem that is manmade or he's just born with it, it's a problem. I believe that horses are students just like people and it takes a good student to be a good horse. The more emotional they are — in a bad way (say, spooky) — that plays a role in what is going to be their general success. You can have a horse that has been mistreated in some way. We run against a lot of problems, from being gate sour to stopping at jumps. There are no tricks, in my opinion. It's just to be an honest rider using proper leg and going forward, weathering the storm. They are going to throw temper tantrums. You learn from experience where the line in the sand is and where you are going to cross. You need to decide to just walk away for that day, or walk away forever. And that's about the horse deciding to be a good student. Most of the time, they respond and you can make them a viable horse for a purpose. Sometimes you run into a horse that is just shutting down to a point that it's not worth going forward."

WORKING WITH YOUNGER HORSES

"The basic bad habits that you find in a young horse are balking or refusing to go forward, whirling — all those green horse-type of things. If you get your legs around them and get them up into your hands, you have a good start.

"Make sure your young horse is ready to work when you're ready to ride. If he is too high, both of you will spend more time just working down, rather than making training progress. Young horses need their turnout so they can get some playfulness out of their system before your training session with them. If we know our young horse is too high to do serious work when we're going to the ring, we'll go ahead and longe him for five to ten minutes to get some of that out before we get on and expect him to be a good student. When you find yourself in a situation that prevents you from longeing, go ahead and ride, just don't expect too much from them for the first ten minutes or so. During that time, put the emphasis on going forward and don't be too demanding with your training expectations.

"When we have a young horse with a poor work ethic and he tends to resist most training, we'll use side reins and longe him before we ride. This gets through those initial confrontations without being in the fight directly, letting them work through their temper. Once they've settled and are going nicely forward in the side reins, then go ahead and give them twenty to thirty minutes of work. If you have one that likes to hesitate at the gate, carry a crop in your outside hand and tap him on the shoulder while you push with your legs. Always use your crop in a reinforcing way in conjunction with your leg and try to use it before the actual disobedience occurs.

"I see a lot of riders who get mesmerized, looking at the horse's head to see if he is framed correctly. The problem with that is, it stops forward motion. Always look up and make sure you're riding leg to hand to create a forward track.

"With young horses, it's important to shift gears smoothly and go through the gears, up and down. This means, let's say when you're cantering, you don't go directly to a walk or halt. Think of going forward while downshifting, so when you're cantering, go to a forward trot then a forward walk, always keeping the horse in front of your leg with your eyes up, and looking ahead to create a track.

"Try not to forget the walk. So many people always walk on the loose rein. Then, when they pick up their reins, the horse gets anxious. Don't forget that the walk is a gait too, and needs to be practiced while going forward into the bridle with good balance and step.

"Don't try to be a hero if your young horses throw a fit and are flinging themselves around to the point of being dangerous. The other day, I was riding a five-year-old, and I knew he was too high, but due to time demands, I'd gone ahead and hopped on. Everything was fine until the person in the ring with me left with his horse. Then, mine went ballistic. He was balking at the gate and rearing every time I would try to make him go away from the gate area. Well, rather than having a knock-down, drag-out fight with him, I hopped off, grabbed a longe line, then took him to the far end of the ring and let him gallop on the longe for five minutes, each way. I got back on and finished with no problems and haven't had one since, with or without another horse in the ring. Thus, what could have been a huge confrontation between my young horse and myself turned into nothing. I got my point across about going away from the gate when I had him in a state of mind to submit without too much energy to successfully fight with me. After that, I did not go straight back to the barn. Instead, I rode him at a walk around the farm, praising him for being brave and independent. I try to always end on a good note with a relaxed horse.

"After they lose a couple of temper tantrums and they realize that you're still going to be up there and they're still going to go forward, they give in. If you win the battle and get your point across, you try not to go back there again. With some young horses, I try not to ride them directly back to the barn. On young horses, I will teach riding lessons, teach over jumps, and bring them with me and have them with me the whole time just to have them get used to being out of their stalls and around the noise of poles dropping and horses rushing past them.

When you get into the real complicated ones that want to be very self-destructive fighting you, you have to decide if the price to fix them is worth it. Picking fights doesn't work. You have to make them go forward. Forward is the key. Too much hand too soon and not enough leg is often the problem. Legs make the pressure on those hands. Obviously, if you're riding a horse in the first month of his riding career, you can't expect him to understand this. Horses find confidence and security in people who are decisive but fair. You give them good grooming, you handle them in the barn, and you don't expect them to misbehave in the barn. You expect general obedience when you load them and lead them and during barn handling. They learn not to step out of line, and to behave themselves, or they are disciplined for it. When you get one that's spoiled, you just treat them fair and ride them fair."

JUMPERS

"When it comes to jumping technique and the finer points of taking a horse that's a 7 Jumper and making it a 9 or 9½ Jumper (moving from high level jumping competition to the upper echelon), or one that gets heavy in the corners or one that rushes a jump late in the round — those are the ones we work on. It costs just as much to show or feed a bad horse. They all have to be physically sound. But, then it comes down to, are they a good student? Can they concentrate? Do they look forward to going to the ring? Do they have a good attitude about new jumps and new experiences? Life is a lot easier for a horse that wants to do his job.

"Rebel's Run [an Irish Draught Sport Horse who started competing in Jumpers with Kels aboard] flourished with us because we allowed him to express himself. He just had an immense amount of curiosity and no fear of anything. That's how, at 15.2 hands, he was able to do Grand Prix and do junior jumpers. His bravery and his heart were incredible."

HUNTER CHALLENGE

"Some show hunters are better if they never see the ring. Others won't jump the third fence if they don't get in and hack around. Both can be winners. The one that's the innate jumper, the one that likes to go out and jump the new jumps, is going to be more successful. A horse that must be longed and hacked prior to going into the show ring is likely going to have much worse x-rays at the age of ten (because they require training that is far more punishing on their bodies and joints to get the same result as a horse that easily tackles requests without such taming, fixing and/or anxiety). That's why the innate jumpers are the much more expensive horses.

"We had a gray mare that was the type that you needed to get tired to not blow up in the ring, but it wasn't necessary to take her in the ring. She always jumped her best the first time at a new fence. Sometimes, when you were riding her to the show ring from the barn area, out of the blue, she'd go straight up, whirl, and try to run back to the barn. When you get those, you just need to know where that line in the sand is and you try not to cross it. It didn't matter what you did in the extreme either way (through praise or punishment). She would not move unless it was going back to the barn. If you forced the issue, the only answer was going straight up in the air. With those types, you need to be very careful. You can still win a lot with them, but knowing the horse over time with experience and knowing what to do and what not to do is important with the particular horse. She was a very honest mount. In the show ring, over the year we had her, she finished top ten in the nation in the Older Small Junior Working Hunter Division.

About Mike Bonham

Mike Bonham has been actively training and showing in the horse business for thirty years. Bonham Stables has turned out hundreds of AA Hunter Champions and multiple Grand Prix Champions under Mike's training. Kels Bonham won the Medals in 2008, and at age fourteen was an individual Bronze Medalist at Prix de States at Harrisburg (that is the Junior Jumper National Championship). Mike admits he found his niche when his kids came along. Kels is a talented rider who has spent many years showcasing horses in training and in competitions. "When she was ten or eleven years old, she was getting catch rides because she was very serious about what she did and put in the work," Mike explains. "She got a lot of breaks that way and she deserved them. She was a unique student for me, and we reached heights in the sport that we thought we would never reach," he admits. Chester is now riding and showing with Mike.

Mike Bonham
Bonham Stables

mlbonham@live.com

(918) 521-4323

Chapter Eighteen

ROBERT FERA

Robert Fera
Professional stallion handler, breeder
Puslinch, Ontario, Canada

ROBERT FERA IS THE OWNER and manager of Deerpath Breeding and Development in Puslinch, Ontario, Canada. He's spent years managing the reproductive needs of mares and stallions, as well as foaling and foal development. His knowledge and experience has even veterinarians viewing him as a sought-after resource for issues relating to his expertise.

WHAT'S THE REAL PROBLEM?

Robert indicates that "health has a lot to do with a horse's behavior. A lot of people think it is training. The first thing that I always look for in a problem stallion, problem mare, or a foal is: is their problem related to a health issue? Once we can rule out the health-related problems, then we can address the training problem and look at the reason this horse is having an issue.

"Stallions sometimes have ulcers. They are not allowed to play with other horses. There are those stallions out there that are allowed to go out with a herd, but most live a solitary life. Stallions with issues usually stem from gastrointestinal upset and anxiety — a lot really do well when they are put on a probiotic or a gastrointestinal digestive enhancer or even ulcer medication. Sometimes with babies that are acting out — it is a heath issue. So, a lot has to do with health and I look at health first and foremost and then I look at everything else."

Relative to horses misbehaving with handlers, Robert cites a likely horse reaction. "How does this new person fit in with the herd? It's a test. You have to stand tall, go in, and assume control because that horse is going to know that you are assuming the control. If you're going to put your head down and be meek about it, then the horse knows, OK, I can take control. Some horses just need a stern voice. On my staff, I have young girls in their twenties who are great under saddle, but I've also had to give them voice lessons — 'I want you to stand tall and assert your voice. Just stand tall and growl, and that horse will stop'."

DOMINANCE TO THE EXTREME

"I had one stallion in here for collections that was showing at a very high level and had shown internationally. He showed up with a note saying 'don't give eye contact.' And, I was like, what is this? I thought, well this is out of the ordinary. And it was no guff. As soon as I went in the stall and looked at him straight on, he lunged at the stall grill, teeth bared, with a look that said he wanted to kill me. I tried something; he was nice and calm in his stall and I'd walk by with my head down then with my head up and he'd lunge at the grill again. This is a horse that I have to breed, and I can't breed if he feels that he is the dominant one. He had to understand that I was going to protect him, and I'm the one that's going to tell him when to breed and when not to breed. It took about a month to get him slowly used to the fact that I wasn't going to hurt him; and that I can look at him face-to-face. At first, he'd always want to rush. He wanted to run and he was obviously not really well trained in hand. He was uncontrollable and high strung with a lot of anxiety. It took a long, long time just to get it in his head that I will let you do what you want to do, but you can't be stupid about it. Relax. Eventually it worked.

"Drugs, like Valium, also help with those kinds of problems. It's not that you're sedating these horses, but you are taking the anxiety level down. Then, you can take him off the Valium and he's already gotten used to you without the anxiety level. The real reason for a lot of problems is, horses get anxious because they think they're going to get hurt or beat. It almost blows their mind, and they forget everything and get all nervous, and the next thing you know, some people are giving the horse a beating because he's not doing what you wanted him to do. And, if you don't register that as a horse handler or even a rider, that anxiety keeps building until one day it explodes and you have an unruly horse. They just go over the top.

"That's what may have happened with that stallion that I couldn't look in the eye for the first little bit. With anxiety comes gastrointestinal problems and a variety of lashing out. And that goes back to the young horses. If you stress them out and make them anxious, you're not achieving anything.

"If we can make stallions content with respect to nutrition, housing, turnout, exercise, and health management, we will get more out of them. With that also comes a respect for the fact that they are a very proud and noble creature."

TIPS FOR DEALING WITH YOUNG STUDS

"A rambunctious colt to a skillful stallion is what we envision when we see a young colt play and have fun, but how do you turn that ball of hormones into a tall, proud, majestic stallion?" Robert asks.

He calls it "controlled enthusiasm; getting your stud to behave like a stallion naturally in a controlled setting with mutual respect."

"Stallion handlers set the horse's conduct. You must allow the stallion to act like a stallion and even applaud it, but not let him get carried away and put you or he in a dangerous situation. Instilling and reinforcing ground manners at an early age will help later. Young colts need to learn to stand and walk on and back up with command, and yield to lead-shank pressure. The stallion must learn that the handler can stop him and control his direction. Stallions should take their cue from the handler when it is time to collect or mount a mare. A handler's personal space should not be invaded as this can throw a person off balance or put the handler in a situation where they will not be able to control the stallion.

"Stallions will learn through repetition and when a positive routine is established, then the stallion will feel comfortable. Teaching a stallion to perform in the breeding shed, whether for live cover or collections, must be planned. Before you get to the shed, the stallion should have his ground manners in place.

"Stallions will act like stallions and call, prance, curl their upper lip, and get all puffed up. These actions are normal and should not be disciplined, but there are limits to behavior. Stallions should never strike, kick out, rear, or charge for teasing or washing or during the act of mating or collecting. Reprimanding must be done quickly, sometimes with a growl and a *No!*, sometimes with shank pressure and sometimes with a crop. It is important to get to know the stallion as some respond differently. Don't over-reprimand, which could fracture a young stallion's confidence and cause more problems, or even cause a stallion to lose respect for the handler. Misbehaving breeding stallions should be handled by experienced handlers and may require some reschooling. When working with stallions, remember to be fair, firm, and consistent. This leads to respect and an understanding of the requested task.

"When teaching a young stallion to breed, it is important to study his behavior and see his frame of mind. Is he aggressive? Timid? Or, does he fall somewhere in between? Sometimes we must modify our ways in order to get him to do his job. Patience is important when working with young stallions as they look toward you for guidance. Thoughtful handling will lead to mutual respect and less hassle in the breeding shed.

"Training young stallions should not be taken lightly, and should not be done by a novice. The act of stallion collection or live covering a mare is a dangerous act for both the stallion and the breeding team. Controlling a stallion's behavior will help minimize the risk of injury, but won't eliminate it. Each stallion is different and what works for one may not work for others. Adapting breeding shed protocols to each stallion individually allows for higher success rate in completing the job with mutual respect and understanding," Robert concludes.

About Robert Fera

Robert Fera is the owner and manager of Deerpath Breeding and Development in Puslinch, Ontario, Canada. The facility takes in stallions at stud owned by others, provides collection and training services, troubleshoots nutritional challenges for stallions, mares and foals, and provides a resource for those seeking a safe, watchful, and expert environment for births and early foal imprinting.

With his education and experience in animal health, Robert provides professional equine services and works with many veterinarians who both refer to and rely on him for experienced stallion management and foal development.

He is also a published author on such topics as stallion management, foal nutrition, and foal development.

Additionally, Robert provides support to breeders and feed dealers as an equine specialist for an animal nutrition company in Cambridge, Ontario.

Visit his website for more information and instructive articles.

Robert Fera

http://www.deerpathequine.com

Chapter Nineteen

FLEUR BRYAN

Fleur Bryan
British Horse Society certified instructor,
trainer, breeder
Smithfield, Kentucky, U.S.A.

FLEUR HAS OVER TWENTY YEARS experience breaking young horses and retraining problem mounts. While in Ireland, Fleur spent fifteen years breeding, training, and competing show jumping horses. Now based in Kentucky, Fleur breeds top-quality Irish Sport Horses and focuses riding time on turning retired racehorses into hunter/jumpers.

MAN-FEARING IRISH SPORT HORSE GELDING

"Over the years, I have passed many horses through my hands," Fleur explains. "Some stand out for the challenges they pose, or for their achievements. I have always enjoyed taking the horses that 'needed fixing.' They were tough, and required a lot of time and patience, but the rewards can be immense.

"One of my best memories is of a young Irish Sport Horse gelding. His owner came to me and asked if I could help him. I knew the man well and had seen the horse at a younger age, recognizing him as a cracking prospect. Once his story came out, though, it was clear something had gone terribly wrong. His 'instructors' had made some mistakes, and the boy was now unridable. Nobody could even stay on him. Even going in his stall at feed time was dangerous. I wasn't sure what, if any-thing, I could do at this point, but was willing to try to help.

"I took him in and accepted the challenge.

"When he brought me the horse, he said the problem was he wouldn't stop bucking. What he didn't tell me was that he wasn't broke. They'd take him out to soft ground in the middle of a marshy field where the footing was deep and he couldn't buck. He'd be all the way up to his knees and hocks in the mud and had to struggle and drag his legs to get through the muck. They'd just go out and ride him in a straight line. Then someone would turn him around, and they'd do it again. Once they brought him onto regular ground, he started bucking like crazy.

"When I first hopped on his back, there was nothing there when I tried to find brakes or steering. He wasn't even clever enough to catch hold of the bit and pull. He really had no idea how to respond to a rider. When I figured that out, I knew straight away my first job was to completely start from scratch. The problem with that was I had already put the saddle on him, so I had unknowingly broken his trust when he didn't know what he was doing. That was my mistake. Of course, if I had known at this time what this horse had been through earlier — I didn't find out about the marsh until much later — it's a mistake I wouldn't have made. As far as that day was concerned, the only thing to do was to make sure I didn't come off him. I was able to stay with him by leaving him alone and quietly riding straight lines along the arena walls until he settled down. Once he settled down, and he wasn't trying to kill me anymore, I stopped for the day.

"Then, I gave him a couple days off. During this time, we started the process of me hanging out in the stall with him. I was the only one that fed him, the only one that watered him. I'd go in and pick his feet out, brush him down, and let him realize I wasn't going to hurt him.

"I spent the next two days doing nothing but bonding: hand-feeding him, patting his head and neck, and lifting his feet. On day three, the breaking tack went on, and out we went in the long lines. I spent several weeks working quietly on his mouth through the woods, out on the road through traffic, in the arena, and around the jumps, just to rebuild his confidence.

"One evening, I discovered a new problem. I had addressed his mouthing issues and felt we were well on our way to success. Just as I thought we were ready to move on, a man came into the arena. The horse went postal! He was scared of men. The mere sight of a man sent him through a concrete wall. Once I made that discovery, we actually ran into a whole set of new problems. By now, he knew how to snatch up the bit and run blind. So, for the next few days, I enlisted every man I knew to go in his stall and come in the arena while I worked. Only a man provided each meal or treat. Slowly, he began to settle and, within the next week, I was on his back again.

"We had to go back to the drawing board on the taking-hold-of-the-bit situation and teaching him to accept men. Flatwork, including circles, turns, figure eights, and upward and downward transitions were a part of everyday training. This also included lots of half-halts, backing up, and the natural aids of seat, leg, and voice, with quiet hands only being used as a last resort.

"One of the things I discovered was this horse loved to jump. Being introduced to any obstacle was a treat for him, so I came to end every session with some poles. Given his demonstrated fear of men, I'd bring out the jump crew — any man would do — about one-half to three-quarters of the way into the work session. So, a man was now becoming his answer to fun — and his new friend. Once I figured out that he really loved to jump, it provided a great way to get him excited about training. It didn't matter if it was some poles on the ground, cavalletti, or fences; it was the way we ended every session and served as his reward for listening and responding. Some like to hack out. With this horse, once he was done with the poles, he was done for the day.

"For such a big horse, he had a lovely step. The more he settled, the better it got. His talent over fences grew. He was with me for four months.

"I was delighted the day he was purchased by a lady who had come to have a mare bred. She had seen this horse from the start and was amazed by his improvement. She watched me ride him that day and felt confident enough to sit on him straight away. She bought him on the spot for a price at the time that was a fortune, and took him to go amateur eventing. She sent many letters telling me about what a wonderful horse he was and how brave he was across the country. He was one of the many success stories I have had, but undoubtedly one of my favorites," Fleur notes.

On Training

"Fixing a badly trained horse is a very complex job and it's not always successful," Fleur explains. "Sometimes, when you watch people, you don't catch what's really going on. I trained with a German lady. She was a talented classical dressage trainer. On every horse, she always rode with her head at a slight tilt. I finally asked why, and questioned how she could keep a horse so straight without riding the horse out of rhythm or into crookedness with her head tilted that way. She responded 'I'm listening to him.' You've got to listen to your horse, and this goes double for a spoiled one. I don't think there's such a thing as a bad horse. They're created.

"When working with a young or spoiled horse, it is best to remember that, while they do not have a memory, they do work on the art of association. Try to never work them in their pasture. They like routine: feed, work, and relaxation should be performed at the same time every day. Be consistent. Ride at the same time so your horse can associate a particular time with going to work," Fleur advises.

Tack: "I grew up with the old-style breaking rollers. This looks like a big leather surcingle with large rings to run long lines through and slightly smaller rings for the side reins or cross reins that attach to the bit. We put a mouth on a horse by continuously driving in long lines. I like a breaking bit, which is a straight-bar, loose-ring snaffle with three little loose-ring keys in the center of it. This gives the horse something to play with and is a very soft bit. It is, however, a dangerous bit for an amateur to use, because if you fit it too tight or too loose, you will train a horse to put his tongue over the bit. One tool that I've found to be very useful for a horse that has been taught to stick his tongue over the bit is a rubber band. I'll use a wide one to tie his tongue down in a figure-eight fashion. This is preferable to harsh bits with ports."

Backing: "I like to back a horse the first few times in the stall and get my two feet in the irons before I take them out, because if they want to buck and rear they can do it in there and they can crack their heads instead of mine. They won't do it a second time. When dealing with problem horses, if you've gotten to the point where they're starting to trust you, and people in general, you can start on the long line. A spoiled horse usually needs to be long-lined for only a week and then you can get back in the saddle. You're just reaffirming the aids as the long lines act as both your leg and hand and correctly fitting side reins encourage the horse to seek out the bit. They will drop their lower jaw and relax into a frame. Don't work in the turnout field. You lose their trust if you take away their relaxation spot by working in there. I do lots and lots of road work. We'll hack out the road at a walk several miles a day."

Environment: "As far as the environment goes, I like everything to be quiet. When working with a horse that's been spoiled and is in for retraining, I make sure he's stabled facing someone in the barn who is a seasoned and relaxed riding horse."

Handling the crazies: "I spend a lot of time bonding with any horse, but especially one that has been started badly. I've had some that are so messed up you can't even catch them in the stall. I'll stand in the corner of their stall holding their feed bucket and won't move until they come and eat. Some won't come near me for hours, but eventually they'll approach. I'll do that for days. Then I'll rub on them until I can get a halter on them. As soon as I can get a halter on them, I'll take them out on the road for a walk with just the lead line for an hour. The next day, the breaking roll goes on in the stall. Then, I'll teach them things like how to cross tie. I do get them to join up with me, but not in the round pen. When I am finished playing with a horse, they will follow me around without a lead on. This is what happens when you build a horse's trust.

"I had one Thoroughbred horse come through my hands going back about ten years ago. She was trained to race and had run. When she came to us, she was virtually unridable. She was a head case. She had no brain. I decided, along with my dad, that we would start her with the usual bonding and long lining. This mare was such a freak show that she actually jumped over a hedgerow in the long lines to get away from me. I could never get her to settle down. There was no reasoning with this horse. My feeling, and I know where she came from and it would surprise me if I was right, but my gut told me she was badly beaten and abused. She didn't trust anybody. It didn't matter if it was male or female. She had no work ethic. You know how some horses are always willing to please, even if they have been spoiled? You can always find a common ground if you use reverse psychology. You could almost make them think it was their idea to go over that jump. She had none of it. She was the kind of horse that wouldn't even take a treat out of your hand.

She was the first one that I could actually say got the better of me and I had to give up. I will say, I did spend close to fifteen weeks working with her before I said this is going nowhere. She was only four. It was very sad. What was even sadder was that her dad was a European Triple Crown winner. It's funny, because a lot of his stock finished up being nasty pieces of work. I didn't find that out until later when I was following the sales in Europe.

"Sometimes, it is in the bloodlines. I knew another Thoroughbred stallion like that. All his foals had a favorite trick. You'd be coming down to a fence with them, and two strides out the sucker would drop the left shoulder and duck. They all did the exact same thing, duck out to the left side, and dump your ass on the floor.

"I will say, though, I learned more off that Thoroughbred mare than I learned off a lot of the good horses. I learn from my mistakes. I've have had very few failures, but you remember them."

The voice: "It's very important to get a horse used to your voice first. Once you start to train him to longe or long line, especially a horse that's been really screwed up or excessively trained in the round pen — there's been overuse of the round pen, particularly in the United States – making your voice a part of the training regimen is important. If you get them used to your voice and tones it's much easier to teach them to longe using voice commands. Once they've got the tones of your voice down and they know whether you're asking them to go forward or come back, and understand what they're supposed to be doing, you can ask them to halt while they stay on the circle. This makes it easier to train the square halt for dressage. This is especially important when you start long lining a horse, because you don't want to put pressure on his mouth. Use your voice the first few days."

The leg: "I'm vertically challenged. I have a strong leg but I do not have a long leg. So, I have to ride a horse onto my leg as opposed to pushing with my leg. Using upward and downward transitions, I actually ride the horse back to me. Circles, turns, figures — anything that is nice and easy but encourages the horse to be responsive — are good ideas."

Horsemanship: "Be patient, quiet, and consistent. Be kind but firm. Always remember you can lead the horse to water but you can't make him drink."

About Fleur Bryan

Fleur is a British Horse Society certified instructor. Before moving to the United States, Fleur owned and managed Barrowside Stud and Equestrian Centre in Ireland. At this facility, she stood six stallions and broke more than forty horses a year.

Fleur has trained with some of the best. While working with the legendary Iris Kellett, she not only learned fine horsemanship but also the art of training the jumper. Fleur credits renowned dressage trainer/judge Gisela Holstein with the influence that governs her approach to flat work and its uses in jumping, through teaching her to sit quietly, have a light hand, and listen to and understand horses.

Her dad taught her everything she knows about breaking young horses. He's her constant mentor, still providing advice long distance from Ireland with the tough ones.

Fleur frequently gives combined training clinics throughout the country and has set up a series of seminars based on Horse Knowledge Care and Riding. She specializes in young or nervous riders and difficult horses. At Parkmore Stud, she breeds top quality Irish Sport horses and stands Parkmore Pride RID, a purebred registered Irish Draught.

Fleur Bryan

http://www.parkmorestud.com
fleur@parkmorestud.com

cell: (502) 649-2037

GETTING
PRACTICAL

A Horse Sense and Cents™ series book wouldn't be complete without discussing sense, cents, and the rewards. The following pages provide some tips, ideas, cautionary notes, and insights for assessing the situation and preparing for your journey with a challenging horse. If you're looking for ideas to get started and budget-conscious suggestions for tools you can use, you'll find them here. The final chapter gives you a glimpse of what the future might hold for you and your mount. It's rarely the outcome that's most significant when you decide to take on a challenging horse but, instead, the process. I encourage you to make the experience more about learning and less about benchmarks. After all, how often do our most memorable equine moments involve the destination?

Chapter Twenty

SENSE

IT'S EASY TO GET CAUGHT up in the challenge of working with a horse you are determined to win over — and fall in love with him in the process. Sometimes you triumph. The victories borne from a patient, attentive, creative, and determined stance — developing a communications process that suddenly turns a difficult horse into an eager and steadfast companion for life — is an experience so rich and rewarding it defies words. The first time this happens, you will forge a bond with your horse you never thought possible — and have a loyal companion that will excel beyond your dreams, simply because you ask. This is an event I hope each of you realize sometime during your life. It is a spiritual experience.

Know, though, that major behavioral issues are best addressed when a horse is relatively young. Not all horses can be turned. If you are faced with a mount that had a bad start under saddle, get him while he's young, as turning is best done before time and mileage have ingrained actions into habit.

Most of the examples provided in this book involve horses that are under five years old. If you have a dangerous horse that is older, consider how much time and money you want to invest in a project that may not have a good outcome. Sometimes it's best to gain some objective perspective, guidance, and supervision from a seasoned and trusted trainer.

Before you take on a difficult project, think about what you want in the end. If the horse you have now is unlikely to get there, perhaps it's time to consider a more suitable mount.

Tackling the challenges of a horse that has been taught to misbehave requires care and precaution. Simple safeguards are vital. Ensure you have control of the horse's head when entering the stall, doing groundwork, or introducing him to anything new. Always put yourself between your equine and an exit when working on an unfamiliar or challenging issue.

Round pens are great for initial assessment and early communication. You can use this tool with or without a longe line, but if the former is the case, be mindful of where the line is and if the horse is considering a change of direction (more on working on the longe and in the round pen is covered in *Horse Sense and Cents: Don't Get Thrown Starting Horses Under Saddle*). Getting twisted in the line can be dangerous for both you and the horse. If you opt for round penning without a line, carry a twenty-foot whip. While not intended for use on the horse, this will be a helpful tool in encouraging the horse to understand requests to move forward and can also serve as a way to drive a threatening horse away.

Wear a hard hat. No matter how skilled you are, these horses are particularly unpredictable, and it only takes one bad fall to learn a very hard lesson — for life.

While it is wise to always make sure someone is around when working with your horse, this isn't always possible. Still, you should at least call someone prior to starting a working session with your troubled horse with an estimated time of completion to call them back. That way, if something does happen, at least someone knows where you are and will get help to you relatively quickly.

Footwear is critical with these challenging steeds. Never wear anything that may get hung up in the stirrup. If you've ever been dragged, you've learned this lesson the hard way and will likely never repeat the transgression. If not, learn from the mistakes of others.

In general, it makes sense to figure out whether your horse prefers routine or needs dynamic lessons to keep it interesting. When dealing with challenging horses, it's best to understand your equine's preferred training and learning style and stick with it until you gain some successes. Catering to the comfort zone of your mount, with an eye toward how you structure your plans to transform his mindset, can be a huge time-saver and an aid in gaining trust and understanding. Early wins are great for both you and the horse, and you should do all you can to try to make that happen. This entire process is a listening exercise. Know early if you and your project are up to the task with this simple assessment goal.

If you find yourself going backward, then regroup, reassess, and alter course. While turning a horse is challenging, lessons should at least end where you started — improvement is not a necessity but losing progress is an indication something is wrong. Of course, you'll have occasional days where there is a distinct failure to communicate. If this becomes a pattern for more than a few days, however, be concerned. Either you have failed to effectively reach your project, or he's not open to change. There's nothing wrong with redirecting your energy and focus by trying a new approach and set of tasks that could net more success. Of course, where Alphas are concerned, you better finish the lesson of the day and win, or your problems will escalate tomorrow. Be smart and resolve to face tomorrow with a better plan for a cooperative end.

Sad as it is, sometimes it's best to simply admit defeat. The headache and heartache that comes from a stubborn conviction to fix a horse that is not receptive to this idea is immense. Know when you're facing a losing battle and have the courage to admit it. There are times when finding a new home for a project that's not working is the best decision for both you and the horse. You may miss the horse for awhile, but soon you will relish your improved quality of life. Use the lesson as a learning experience to ensure your replacement is more suitable — and fun.

Picking the right project is half the battle. Before you embark on this challenging journey, make sure you have the skills and confidence to do what is necessary to help your mount transform. It's also wise to get some objective perspective relative to your horse, goals, and plan from a seasoned trainer. Don't be afraid to ask for assistance. Sometimes, though, that help can interfere with your progress. If someone's style is undermining your achievements, find another who is more compatible with you and your horse.

When you find the right horse and muster the patience and persistence to turn him into a wonderful partner, it will change your life. If you need some help along the way or want to shout about your victories, don't hesitate to contact us through our website, http://www.HalcyonAcres.com, or through our blog, http://www.HorseSenseandCents.com.

Chapter Twenty-One

CENTS

MONEY IS AN ISSUE WITH the typical horse owner, and this can be a big factor with problem horses. Sometimes it comes down to throwing good money after bad. Try not to look at what you've invested, but instead, what you can hope to achieve. With a good horse or a bad one, you still have the expense of feeding and housing the animal — not to mention your time and energy put forth to care for and train him. Consider the cost of time, frustration, and support needed to fix a horse that has major problems. While a successful project may net a competitive or companion horse far more loyal and more of a standout than a made horse, you'll likely lose months or even years of opportunity to enjoy the horse for your intended use. There is a cost beyond the cash, too. It makes sense to proceed if you are making headway while gaining satisfaction and knowledge as you work with your project. If, however, you are growing tired and weary of even going to the barn to face your mount, it might be time to cut your losses. Problem horses are challenging for even the most seasoned riders. Sometimes they're worth the time and expense — other times, not. Be ready to bail if the fun is gone from your equine interactions.

Before you embark on a turning strategy, it might make sense (and save cents) to have a professional provide some input. Conformation, soundness, surefootedness, carriage, athleticism, attitude, size and, in some cases, appearance, all play a role in whether your intended mount will be able to meet your long-term expectations. These are traits any qualified trainer can assess and address. If you've bought or inherited a problem horse, it's likely your journey will be a long one, and it's smart to first determine if there's a possibility of getting to where you want to go.

If you decide to send your mount to another for training, determine up front a reasonable timeframe for progress with some benchmarks for success. The bill can mount quickly, and it's important to set some limits on how long you are willing to invest in the project prior to seeing some results. What are your goals, and what achievements would indicate your horse is moving toward them in a reasonable amount of time? Granted, it's usually a lot tougher, and more time-consuming, to turn a horse than to start them right in the first place, but you should decide what constitutes a reasonable decision period to proceed. If you've found a competent trainer, it should be clear in the first thirty to sixty days if this horse is reachable. Subsequent riding lessons for you on your horse are critical for long-term success. If your chosen turning facility is too far away to work with you in person, they should be available to troubleshoot issues via phone or e-mail — and adept at interpreting the problem and explaining how to resolve it remotely. If no progress is cited and more time is required after sixty days, this may not be a good investment.

The do-it-yourself method can be rewarding and cost-effective — if you are making progress. You can save a lot of time and money (don't forget, though, vet bills and human injury recovery costs can be considerable if you're not smart about safety) by investing in some basic equipment. Round pens can be built with lumber or purchased as portable metal units. The latter is fairly expensive. Having a small, circular space to begin ground training is the most effective way to assess and control your horse. Setting the stage will have a considerable impact on your outcome. This should be at least fifty feet in diameter with sixty feet being ideal. Any smaller and the space becomes too difficult for your horse to keep his balance at progressive gaits and too close-quartered for you to maintain safety. Too much bigger and you lose your ability to dictate the horse's movements — which is the objective of starting training in the round pen. Often it is easier to work with a horse on a longe line initially, disconnecting it after you establish a communications system. A twenty-foot line with an accompanying twenty-foot whip works well in this space.

Round pen training should be relatively short in duration and something you strive to move away from as quickly as possible. Besides the unnatural physical demands it puts on the horse at faster paces, the closed environment limits exposure to the varied sights, sounds, and terrain a horse will be required to accept. This can be an ideal environment for establishing initial body language and voice cues, but it shouldn't be the primary long-term training ground.

Long lines are a great way to get out and about without creating an unsafe situation on the back of a reactionary horse. Outfitting a horse to drive with long reins (lines) can be relatively inexpensive. A good surcingle can be used for many other applications and is a smart investment. You're going to need a bridle and suitable bit anyway for when you hop aboard, so this part of the equipment requires no additional expense. Leather lines that buckle easily to the bit are best. You should have at least eight feet of length extending beyond the horse's body to maintain safety and make this an effective instrument.

Other useful inexpensive tools include:

• a black rubber tie with double-ended snaps on each side

• a leather halter

• a chain to be attached to the end of the longe line and/or lead shank

• a crop or dressage whip

• an old saddle (trees get broken — best not to start with your expensive show saddle — just make sure your tack fits the horse properly)

• a snaffle bit — preferably a full cheek or copper roller

• large or breakaway stirrup irons

• leather reins

• a yoke or martingale without the attachments to the bridle or reins

• and courage and stamina.

It is not wise to get carried away with fancy trimmings when working with problem horses. More equipment can lead to more entanglements. Expensive tack gets broken. In time, you can outfit them with the best, but until you gain a rapport and log some wins, it's bright to be minimalist and focus purchases on the practical tools you need to get the job done.

Chapter Twenty-Two

THE REWARDS

ONCE YOU HAVE EXPERIENCED THE process of successfully turning a problem horse, you will look back on the achievement — and the various challenges and rewards along the way — for a lifetime. Being able to accomplish such a feat not only helps you learn a great deal about horses and how to reach them, but will also teach you a lot about yourself.

The experience will either make you open to another project — or provide the resolve that once is enough. These critters can try your patience, threaten your well-being, and certainly prove costly along the way. Still, the connection you make with a horse deemed unsuitable for riding but that has been turned into a willing, confident, and affectionate companion is incredible. Over time, these horses will generally perform for others as requested, but their response to you will be to give a little more, to try a little harder, and to seek your approval and appreciation with every challenge.

Even walking away serves its own reward. It takes a lot of courage and confidence to admit defeat — and it can definitely be a factor with any of these troubled equines. While the initial decision is a tough one, the time, relief, and quality of life you gain back once they are gone will surprise you. Like a bad relationship, getting into a daily grind with a bad equine not open to your efforts saps your energy and sullies your spirit.

If you find the right horse and the key to reaching him, you'll have stories to tell that will have others laughing out loud, in jaw-dropping awe, concerned for your well-being, ready to shed tears in sympathy, and smiling over what you and your equine have become. You'll also have the satisfaction of a connection with an animal deeper than you ever dreamed possible. Climbing into the saddle or just spending time on the ground with your friend will generate treasured moments and memories far more meaningful than any prior equine achievement.

Enjoy the ride!

GLOSSARY

Aids

Everything you do on your horse's back is an aid, or cue, to the horse to do something he thinks is being suggested – whether you intend it or not. Your seat, leg, hand, body position, and voice are all cues for the horse that he will try to respond to. Know what you're doing with all of your body when your horse doesn't do what you want before you blame him for disobedience.

Allowance company (allowance races)

This is a racetrack term that applies to the level of competition in a race. Most races offer a claiming price for a horse, and any horse entered in that race can be claimed, or bought, for the designated price by another trainer simply submitting a claim form prior to the race start (whether the owner would like to sell the horse or not). Allowance horses tend to be of a much higher caliber than the majority of horses running at a track (with stakes races – included in this designation are the Triple Crown Races – being the only higher designation).

Backing

The term, for the purposes of this book (unless it is obvious the meaning is to go backwards), pertains to getting on a horse's back and generally refers to early lessons when a horse is ridden for the first few times.

Bars of the mouth

This is a sensitive area of the mouth along the gumline where there are no teeth. If you have a bit in his mouth and jerk down on a high head, or up on a low one, you'll likely hit the bars of the mouth and cause the horse some shooting pain. It's important that you fit bits correctly so you don't punish a horse when he is responding. For a horse that is ignoring your hands, a wrap on the bars of the mouth will get his attention quickly, but be ready for a possible dramatic reaction.

Bellied (belly over, bellying over)

When starting a young horse, sometimes the toughest thing for him to deal with is a rider towering over his head. It can also be dangerous to swing a leg over the top of a saddle on a horse that has never felt a leg tickling his sides or the full weight of a rider. Bellying over a horse involves lying across the saddle with your feet on the left side of the horse, your hips straddling the saddle and your upper body either parallel to the ground or lying over the right side of the horse (progressing to the latter in varying stages as the horse indicates he's ready). This approach to introducing a horse to a rider's weight for the first time not only offers a less intimidating initial lesson(s), but also allows the rider to quickly and safely slide off the horse if he panics or rebels.

Block

This is also known as a mounting block. Functions as a stool to raise a rider off the ground to more easily reach the stirrup prior to mounting a horse. This device usually has two steps and is positioned on the left side of the horse while he stands.

Breeze (work, workout)

This is a racetrack term that describes timed sprints performed in the morning (and recorded for bettors to see in the afternoon or evening racing program) to help condition and prepare a racehorse for an upcoming race.

Cavalletti

Poles placed on the ground parallel to each other at various feet measurements (depending on the gate and the intended lesson), either alone or in combination with jumps.

Claimed (in a claiming race)

This is a racetrack term that indicates a horse in a race has been bought by a new owner. In lower level races, horses entered are eligible to be bought, whether the owner wants to sell or not. Claiming races put a price tag on every horse entered (the harder the race, the higher the price — e.g., a $4,000 claiming race means a horse entered in that race can be bought at that price by any eligible individual prior to the start of the race). When a horse is claimed in a race, it means another trainer put in a "claim slip," which makes him (or one of his clients) the new owner of the horse. Hence, the horse is claimed.

Clocker's stand

This is a racetrack term that refers to the building that houses the individual designated to time morning workouts. This building is raised above the ground so that the clocker can see the entire racetrack from this vantage point.

Collections/collecting (sperm collecting)

Stallions that are not exclusively doing live cover (where they physically breed the mares they are inseminating) need their semen collected so it can be chilled or frozen to be sent to mare owners who have selected the stud for their foal sire. This requires a system and a process whereby the stallion breeder (or his vet) induces the stallion to ejaculate into a container housed in a device designed to simulate a mare's cavity.

Draw reins

This is a pair of leather straps that are attached to the girth or a martingale, run through the bit on each side, and held in the rider's hands. This is used to position the head of the horse by applying pressure to the mouth to discourage him from raising his head and/or to force him to bend at his poll (the point on the neck just behind the ears).

Driving lines

These are very long reins (usually leather) that attach to the bit, run through a surcingle (or the stirrups of a saddle if the horse is tacked), and extend behind the horse for steering or stopping from the ground. They're a good tool for working with a horse that is learning to handle tack, and ultimately, a rider, and also effective with equines that have issues. Make sure you keep yourself out of harm's way when working with this tool by traveling a safe distance behind, or to the side of, the horse. Equines that have not been properly introduced to objects touching their hindquarters may panic when the reins are brought to their rear and/or touch their haunches.

Eventing (event)

This is a three-phase competition that includes dressage, cross-country (jumping across terrain over miles that usually includes woodland, fields, hills, water, and a variety of challenging obstacles and approaches) and stadium (similar to show jumping). At the higher levels, this is held over a three-day period. Some use the term "three-day eventing" even when referring to lower levels that occur over the period of a day or two.

FEI

The Fédération Equestre Internationale (FEI), founded in 1921, is the international body governing equestrian sport recognized by the International Olympic Committee (IOC). It is based on the principle of equality and mutual respect between all 134 affiliated National Federations, without prejudice to race, religion, or internal politics. The FEI is the sole controlling authority for all international events in Dressage, Jumping, Eventing, Driving, Endurance, Vaulting, Reining, and Para-Equestrian. It establishes the regulations and approves the equestrian programs at Championships, Continental and Regional Games, as well as the Olympic Games.

First Level Dressage

Dressage is a discipline where horse and rider work together to perform various moves on the flat that culminate in specific tests that are ridden in competition. "The purpose of the First Level Dressage Tests is to confirm that the horse, in addition to the requirements of Training Level, has developed thrust (pushing power) and achieved a degree of balance and throughness. Trot work on ten-meter circles and twenty-meter serpentines is added, as well as lengthened trots first rising, and later at sitting trot; the remainder of trot work is done sitting. Canter work is on fifteen-meter circles and straight lines, with lengthening also introduced at the canter. Leg yield and change of canter lead through trot are also introduced by the end of the First Level tests." (Source: USEF Rulebook)

Flatwork

Any under-saddle work that does not involve jumping fences, speed training, or other gymnastic training activity.

Flipping (flip)

Some horses that rear also flip over. This occurs when they get past perpendicular to the ground and fall backwards or sideways, landing either on their back or side, respectively. This is an extremely dangerous behavior. Even an experienced rider can easily get pinned under such a horse and incur serious injuries from the impact and weight of the horse on top of them. Sometimes it's intentional, but usually not. A rider who does not have the balance to stay with a known rearer (and, consequently, is likely to pull them over onto their backs or sides by using the reins to try to keep themselves on the horse or losing their balance and tipping them over) should never get on one.

Flying changes (flying lead changes)

Usually requested during a change of direction, and always involving a canter or gallop pace, this comes from a rider cue that asks the horse to change both front and hind leads simultaneously. A horse is most balanced when cantering or galloping on what is called the correct lead, which has the outside front leg making the first stride, but the inside leg performing a much longer stride and is referred to as the right or the left lead, corresponding with the direction the horse is tracking.

Forehand turns (turn on the forehand)

This is a movement, cued by rider hand, leg, and seat aids (and sometimes with other aids from a handler on the ground) whereby the horse rotates his hind legs around forelegs that remain in the same position.

French Link bit

The French Link is a small, flat, peanut-shaped link in the center of the mouthpiece (creating two joints). It lays flat to the bit. The French Link doesn't have the nutcracker action of a single jointed snaffle and therefore may be a good choice for horses with a low palate. Instead, the mouthpiece lays flat across the tongue. There is a lot more mobility within the mouthpiece, so some horses that may get "set" in a single-jointed bit go lighter and lean on the bit less. It should be noted that horses with large or sensitive tongues may not like the French Link snaffle because of the close contact of the bit with the tongue.

Gap

A racetrack term that refers to areas along the exterior perimeter of the track that have been selected as designated entry and exit points from the barn area for morning training. These involve breaks in the otherwise continuous metal or wood circumference barrier. Gaps are closed during racing hours, usually with an inserted steel attachment, to prevent horses competing in races from seeing the opening and deciding to go home prior to finishing the race.

Get topside

This is a British term that refers to a belligerent horse and usually involves him trying to mow you over, rear, strike, or behave in a manner that puts his body over yours during handling exercises.

Ghosts

Horses that spook for no reason or get terrified with no cause are sometimes described as seeing ghosts.

Groundwork

Groundwork is everything from leading and grooming to long lining and work in the round pen. Anything you do on the ground will help — or hinder — your communications with the horse once you get on their backs. When dealing with a horse that already has issues, it is very important to be clear and insistent about your communications in all you do on the ground.

Hack

This refers to a calm, relaxed, and quiet ride that can be on the trails, around the property, or on the roads.

Half halt (half halting)

A half halt is a closing of the fingers on the reins to cue a horse to an upcoming request, to slow the pace, or to soften his mouth. This is a light cue that involves an immediate release.

Half-mile gap

Most racetracks have horse paths leading from the backside, where horses are stabled, to the track for training in the morning that includes a gap in the normally continuous outside rail. Often, these entrance and exit gaps are at the half-mile pole, or the midway point to the finish line. These gaps are open in the morning during training hours and closed off with a metal rail inserted across the area during afternoon races.

Hand

This is a standard measurement that denotes the size of the horse, measured from the withers. One hand is equivalent to four inches, so a 15-hand (also designated as 15hh) horse would be five feet from the ground as you stand at their shoulder and look at the highest point of the withers (at the bottom of the neck).

Hang (rear and hang)

When a horse rears and holds a position perpendicular to the ground for more than a few seconds, this is called hanging.

Hay net

This is a bag with large holes in it, often made of cotton or nylon rope and tied in a fashion to hold hay, but provide the horse with ample opportunity to remove hay at will. Hay nets have a long rope which threads through holes at the top of the bag to tie it up so that hay can be easily reached when a horse is tied. These devices also keep hay off the ground, reducing worm re-infestation and providing a way to offer horses hay all the time with reduced waste that would occur if this quantity of hay were provided on the floor of the stall (where the horse would likely soil it after a couple of hours with their waste).

Heart

Horses that are termed to have heart possess willpower, determination, and gumption well beyond the norm. These horses can fight you to exhaustion but, if you gain their respect, will also surprise you by giving 110% every time you ask for more than they should be able to muster. Heart is inborn and a product of genetics.

Herd bound (nappy)

Horses that refuse to leave the barn or the facilities where they are housed without a companion horse are termed herd bound or, in England, nappy. This can involve riding activities as well as their willingness to pay attention to you during ground work exercises. Often, these horses will scream for, or at, their companions, run over the top of you, or resort to wheeling or backing as you try to ride them away from the herd. Proper training in the first place and/or subsequent correct handling can help you easily avoid this challenge.

In-hand

When you are holding your horse on the end of a lead rope.

Iron Halter

An iron halter usually has a single leather strap that loops over the poll of the horse (just behind the ears) and a circular or oval steel ring that goes over the nose. This is a very severe device that should only be used with horses that are so dangerous they cannot be controlled in any other fashion.

Lead Pony (pony)

Another primarily racetrack term, this is a horse that has been trained to lead another horse (generally on their right side) at various gates, with or without a rider aboard. If you've ever watched a televised race, you'll note each racehorse is accompanied to the starting gate by another horse and rider. The horses are called lead ponies (even though most are considerably taller than 14.2hh). During morning training hours, a "pony" exercises many horses without a rider aboard. To pony a horse, or be a pony, in this sense, means the equine steed has been taught to be comfortable and tolerant of having a horse attached to them. The good ones have the instinctual smarts to do what is necessary to stick with a racehorse that is difficult. Well-trained and talented lead ponies will respond to rider weight and the behavior of the horse next to him without the need for any rein or leg cues to contain and/or stay with a fractious horse.

Leg up

Good conditioning work requires stretching, building, exercising, and strengthening all the tendons, ligaments, muscles, and bones of a horse with the goal of readying him for competitive or pleasure demands. Legging up a horse provides the foundation strength and flexibility to ensure his legs are ready to handle the rigors of future demands. This is often best achieved through hill work at slower paces.

Many people also shorten the term "getting a leg up" to leg up, which, in this case, refers to assistance mounting a horse where a ground person grasps a rider's left leg (usually at the ankle) to help provide a boost onto the horse.

Lip Chain

This is a chain that is usually at the end of a lead rope, but can also be a separate item, which threads through the left side of the halter, across the top of the gum under the lip and affixes tightly to the right side of the halter. This should only be used in extreme cases and by an experienced horse handler. It can help control a horse (used right, it releases endorphins that serve to relax the horse) that is dangerous or otherwise impervious to standard leading tools. Steady pressure can flip a horse over and is an inappropriate use of the device.

Long line (long lining, long reining)

Think of driving the horse while you stand on your feet (instead of in a cart or carriage). These are extra long reins that attach to the bit, generally run through a surcingle on each side of the horse (or stirrups if you have a saddle on the horse), and are held by a person behind or to the side of the horse (depending on how you are using them). This tool can help to teach a young horse how to steer, stop, and respond to voice commands prior to carrying a rider. It is also helpful in assessing issues with horses that have problems and reestablishing a communications process that is productive and rewarding.

Longe Line (often written Lunge)

A long rope of woven cotton (or nylon, but this is not recommended) that is usually about twenty feet long and used to teach and then exercise a horse in a circle around a human handler. The longe line is a tool best used sparingly as it can put unnecessary stress on a horse's joints, but can be a good tool to begin a communications process, particularly with a horse that tends to view flight as his favorite response to issues.

Longe (often written Lunge) whip

Used primarily on the longe line or in the round pen, this usually has a twenty-foot reach with a six-foot plastic (coated with braided nylon) handle and stick that extends out with a flexible end to encourage the horse to move forward (or maintain direction). This should never be used on the horse, but can be cracked to make a noise to encourage a horse that is not responding.

Lung up

High level competitive horses need to build their lungs to handle the rigors of performance demands. This is often best done through speed work.

Made horse

A made horse refers to an equine mount that has been taught to perform exceptionally, usually even in the face of rider error or interference. These horses are easy to ride and well trained to do the job requested. If the rider is correct in their cues, these horses tend to do exactly what they are asked. Often they'll also step in to fix a rider's mistake.

Martingale (running, standing, German)

This is a device is used to restrict the movement of the horse's head and/or establish more rider control. There are a variety of types of martingales, including: standing (which stops the horse from raising his head past a certain level with a strap that attaches to the noseband, much like a tie down); running (with two rings that run through the reins so the rider's hands control the amount of pressure to the bit — these are often used on horses that tend to run off as the more the rider pulls, the lower the horse's head must go) and German (which attaches to each rein and prevents a horse from raising his head past a certain height).

Neck stretcher

A device made of strong elastic that attaches to the girth and adjusts over the poll. It encourages your horse to drop his head, flex and stretch forward to the bit without encouraging the resistance and resentment of a non-elastic cord.

Overfaced (overfacing)

When horses are introduced to new lessons before they are ready, they lose trust in their rider or handler. Equines that have been overfaced tend to panic in new situations, refuse, and/or develop sour attitudes.

Parking

This is a term that refers to a horse's behavior when they refuse to go.

Passage

The passage is a movement seen in upper-level dressage, in which the horse performs a highly elevated and extremely powerful trot. The horse is very collected and moves with great impulsion. The passage differs from the working, medium, collected, and extended trot in that the horse raises a diagonal pair high off the ground and suspends the leg for a longer period than seen in the other trot types. The hindquarters are very engaged, and the knees and hocks are flexed more than the other trot types. The horse appears to trot in slow motion, making it look as if it is dancing. The passage is first introduced in FEI test Intermédiaire II. A horse must be well confirmed in its training to perform the passage, and must be proficient in collecting while remaining energetic, calm, and supple. The horse must also have built up the correct muscles to do the strenuous movement. (Source: Wikipedia)

Piaffe

The piaffe is a dressage movement where the horse is in a highly collected and cadenced trot, in place or nearly in place. The center of gravity of the horse should be more towards the hind end, with the hindquarters slightly lowered and great bending of the joints in the hind legs. The front end of the horse is highly mobile, free, and light, with great flexion in the joints of the front legs, and the horse remains light in the hand. The horse should retain a clear and even rhythm, show great impulsion, and ideally should have a moment of suspension between the footfalls. (Source: Wikipedia)

Picking feet

Good horse maintenance and proper schooling of young horses requires picking up their feet and using a hoof pick to clean out any debris that may be lodged in the bottom of their hoofs.

Poles

This is a racetrack term that signifies the distance traveled around a track that is typically a mile in length. These are color coded and divided by half, quarter, eight and sixteenth of a mile increments. All poles are distanced from the wire, or finish line.

Ponied

> A horse that is being led by a lead pony (the lead pony has a rider aboard, but the horse being ponied may or may not) is termed being "ponied." The rider on the pony holds onto the head of the horse being ponied, usually with a leather lead, or pony strap. This term does not refer to the height of the horse.

Prix St. George dressage

> The first recognized level (of four) of dressage in FEI (Fédération Equestre Internationale) — international levels.

Quarter mile pole

> This marker, or distance from the finish line, often includes a gap in the exterior perimeter of the racetrack to provide easy access for maintenance equipment, admittance to the paddock for horses coming to race from the backside, and/or to offer a starting gate position during morning training hours for short workout sprints.

Rate

> To rate a horse means that you are modifying his speed (usually requesting a slower pace than he would prefer).

Resistance bands

> People sometimes use these in physical fitness routines. They are elastic in nature and can increase the intensity of a workout. The more pressure you apply to the band (the more you stretch it), the more tension it provides. Some people use these with horses to encourage a particular head set.

Rhythm

> Each horse has his own natural rhythm, which can be described as the beat of the hoofs when he travels in his most comfortable cadence. It's important to establish what this is and how to maintain it before moving on to more difficult requests.

Roll (or surcingle)

> Roll is primarily a European term with the same meaning as a surcingle in the United States. This is a tool,

usually made of leather, which straps around a horse where the saddle would go. It is quite a bit like a continuous girth that goes around the entire circumference of the horse, but with more padding (particularly at the withers) and rings to run long reins and other devices through. It is used with young and troubled horses for groundwork activities in preparation for riding.

Roll-back

A movement where the horse immediately, without hesitation, performs a 180-degree turn after rapidly halting and immediately goes forward again into the original gait. The horse must turn on his hindquarters, bringing his hocks well under himself, and the motion should be continuous, with no hesitation.

Round pen

This is a circular fenced area that is approximately sixty feet in diameter. Various constructions are used including portable gates, wood boards in a typical fencing arrangement as well as lumber creating a solid circumference (generally six feet in height) so that the horse cannot see outside of the working area. The latter generally also includes a deep sand footing.

Shank (lead rope)

This is a cotton rope with a snap, a leather line with a chain, a nylon (not recommended) device with a snap or a chain, or any other tool designed to attach to the halter to lead the horse.

Side-passing

The horse moves sideways with little or no forward motion. This term and movement originated in the cavalry to help correct the spacing of two horses that were side-by-side in a lineup. Today it is seen used in western disciplines, by police horses, and in Doma Vaquera (an equitation style in Spain with roots and contemporary applications to cattle ranching), as examples. This movement teaches the horse to move away from leg pressure.

Side reins

This is a pair of elastic straps that attach to the saddle (or surcingle) on each side of the horse and then to the bit for schooling without a rider. The intended use is to position the horse's head by encouraging (or forcing) him to bend at the poll (the point on the neck just behind the ears).

Six-Furlong gap

A furlong is an eighth of a mile in racetrack terminology. Many mile-long racetracks have an area that extends out from the exterior perimeter at the six-furlong or six-eighths of a mile mark (from the wire). This is due to the fact that this is a common race distance and putting the starting gate at the six-furlong pole would require starting the race on a turn. Consequently, there is often a break in the outside rail at this marker, providing an opportunity for horses that are tracking right to act up in the open area.

Soundness

Horses need to be sound of body and mind to be able to effectively answer your requests. While many limit the definition of an unsound horse to one that moves with a limp, there are many other issues that can impair the horse's ability to perform. There are also horses that do not travel evenly on all four legs that can still step up to their job. When pain is involved, though, it's a problem. If you're looking to buy a horse, or working with one that may be hurting, it's important to have someone available to help you assess and address the issue and determine if it's a concern that could curtail his ability to do what you want.

Soured (sour horse)

Horses that have been taught to hate what their human handler is requiring of them and have no qualms about expressing this are called sour. This can include any number of behaviors, but most involve the horse refusing to do what is requested. The result of forced training when a horse is sore or overfacing a young horse, once a horse reaches this state they are difficult, can be dangerous, and usually require professional intervention.

Horses can also become barn sour or ring sour. The former is often the result of poor early training or an ongoing dependence on other horses. The latter generally occurs when a horse is drilled to resentment without the benefit and relief of varied riding activities.

Spoiled horse

This is a term common in European countries referring to a horse that has been trained badly and is in need of fixing. All the turning projects highlighted in this book could be classified spoiled horses. Some resulting issues are tougher to remedy than others.

Surcingle (roll)

This is a tool, usually made of leather, which straps around a horse where the saddle would go. It is quite a bit like a continuous girth that goes around the entire circumference of the horse, but with more padding (particularly at the withers) and rings to run long reins and other devices through. It is used with young and troubled horses for groundwork activities in preparation for riding.

Sweet-iron

Sweet iron is a dark color and is designed to rust. As it rusts, it produces a sweet taste that horses like.

Tacking

Putting a saddle and/or bridle on a horse.

Tevis Buckle

The prize given for the most famous and arduous 100-mile endurance race in the world, held in New Mexico, U.S.A. Denny Emerson won a Tevis Cup Buckle for completing the 50th anniversary of the Western States Trail Ride.

Three-eighths gap

This is a racetrack term that designates a particular exit or entry area onto the track — in this case, at the three-eighths pole, or three-eighths of a mile from the finish line. Racetracks generally allow training in the morning on the tracks that are used for racing in the afternoon and evening. These tracks are bound by a metal (or, in older cases, wood) perimeter, called a rail, that is closed during racing hours (because horses generally come onto the racetrack from the paddock or "frontside" during live racing). In the morning, horses housed on the "backside," or where the stable area is located, need to get on or off the track to come from or go back to the barns where they live.

Throughness/through

This is a term used primarily in Dressage circles to describe when a horse is giving in the jaw and at the poll while engaging from behind.

Warmbloods

While many breeds and breed crosses can be called warmbloods (as opposed to, for example, hot-blooded Thoroughbreds or Arabs), this term is most often used to designate horse breeds and bloodlines (generally of German or Dutch descent) that are known for their competitive performance prowess.

INDEX

ABOUT THE AUTHOR

Nanette Levin contracted the horse bug early — and whined so much her parents pulled out all the stops to find a training stable for her. They figured an eight-week program would put an end to the five-year-old's whim. They were wrong.

Over the past forty years, Nanette has spent almost every day on a horse — or twenty. Whether competing, starting young horses under saddle, galloping race horses, reeducating stressed and confused equines, preparing horses for new careers, or just enjoying a trail ride, she has found these four-legged companions to be her mainstays. She's worked with people, too, as a respected, appreciated and accomplished stable manager, riding instructor, horse trainer, and equine organization president. Nanette has started hundreds of horses under saddle and works with a growing number of last-chance cases to help them find a new and happier reality.

Today, she owns Halcyon Acres®, a 117-acre facility located in the New York Finger Lakes region, where she breeds Irish Draught Sport Horses and Thoroughbreds. She also oversees all training activities, focusing on starting young horses under saddle and reprogramming uncooperative and/or dangerous horses that have been started badly. She is recognized as a regional go-to resource for working with challenging horses no one else can reach.

Nanette is also a seasoned writer, reporter, and columnist. Her more than twenty-five years as a paid contributor to local and national publications offered many opportunities for equine assignments. She enjoyed getting to know so many readers during her years as a monthly, featured columnist for *Today's Horse Trader,* where she specialized in issues associated with young and challenging horses. Keep an eye out for future articles and features in horse- and rider-focused magazines.